68

D1461791

EMERALD GUIDES

A BUSY MANAGERS GUIDE TO MANAGING STAFF
How to Manage Problem Staff Successfully

Lynda Macdonald

Withdrawn
From Stock

Emerald Publishing
www.emeraldpublishing.co.uk

Emerald Guides
Brighton BN2 4EG

© Lynda Macdonald 2008

All rights reserved. No part of this publication may be
reproduced in a retrieval system or transmitted by any means,
electronic or mechanical, photocopying or otherwise, without the
prior permission of the copyright holders.

ISBN 184716 058 1
ISBN 13: 978184716 058 4

Printed by Biddles Ltd Kings Lynn Norfolk

Cover design by Bookworks Islington

Whilst every effort has been made to ensure that the information
contained within this book is correct at the time of going to
press, the author and publisher can take no responsibility for the
errors or omissions contained within.

LEICESTER CITY LIBRARIES	
125	
Bertrams	30.06.08
658.3045	£9.99

CONTENTS

INTRODUCTION

5

7

INTRODUCTION

This book is intended to be a practical guide for managers as to how to deal with a range of problems associated with employees' behaviour, attendance, performance and general conduct at work. Managers of all levels within all sizes and types of organisation will benefit from reading the pages that follow, which are designed to provide a straightforward and intelligible explanation of relevant employment law and practical, hands-on guidance as to how to deal with problem people at work.

The term "manager" is used throughout the book for convenience and is intended to cover anyone who manages, supervises or is otherwise responsible for the work of other people. This includes departmental managers, section heads, middle managers, junior managers, supervisors, team-leaders, charge-hands, foremen /women etc.

Whenever an employee is promoted to a job that involves the management or supervision of other staff, that individual will, for the first time, become responsible not only for their own work output and conduct, but also for the performance and conduct of other staff. Managers stand to be judged not only on their own personal performance, but also on account of the performance of the staff whom they manage. This principle holds good irrespective of the level of management that the individual has reached, whether as a first level team leader or senior manager. Getting results through other people is the key to success in management, and to achieve this success it is necessary for anyone in a managerial position, at whatever level, to acquire a range of "people management" skills. These skills must include the knowledge and skills needed to deal with staff whose conduct, performance or attendance falls below an acceptable level or starts to cause specific problems.

After chapter 1 of the book which provides a general introduction to managing staff and its associated problems, the book goes on during chapters 2, 3 and 4 to discuss employee misconduct, ranging from commonplace issues such as unsatisfactory timekeeping or poor attitude through to more serious problems such as harassment and stealing. All the necessary and appropriate procedures are explained. Similarly, chapter 5 addresses the subject of managing unsatisfactory job performance, whilst chapters 6 and 7 deal with managing attendance and absence (long-term ill-health absence and frequent short-term absences respectively). Chapter 8 provides a full explanation and clear guidelines on how to dismiss staff fairly, including the procedures that must be followed. Finally, chapter 9 deals with the implementation of necessary changes to employees' terms and conditions of employment and the legal implications of change, together with an explanation of the legality and likely fairness of dismissals on grounds other than conduct and capability.

The law referred to in this book is up-to-date as of March 2008.

CHAPTER 1
MANAGING PEOPLE AND THE ASSOCIATED PROBLEMS

INTRODUCTION

Whenever people are employed, those whose job it is to manage their work output, general performance, attendance and conduct will inevitably face problems from time to time. People are not perfect and there will be many differences between individuals as regards their skills, abilities, levels of motivation, strengths and weaknesses, personalities and general attitude at work.

The Types of People Problems that Managers Typically Face

Some of the common people problems that managers typically face include:

- Unsatisfactory timekeeping;

- Unauthorised absence, ranging from an over-stretched lunch break to complete days off without permission;

- Poor work output, either in terms of quantity or quality;

- Frequent mistakes in a particular employee's work;

- Breaches of the organisation's rules, for example health and safety rules or rules on the use of company resources;

- Aggressive, uncooperative or otherwise unacceptable behaviour;

- A refusal to cooperate with a manager's reasonable instructions;

- Personality clashes;

- Constant complaining or finding fault with everything;

- Lack of certain key skills, for example organisational skills or communication skills;

- General laxness towards, for example, deadlines, dress codes, customer requirements;

- Excessive untidiness;

- Carelessness.

This list is, of course, not exhaustive.

WHY MANAGERS OFTEN FAIL TO TACKLE PEOPLE PROBLEMS

There are a number of common reasons why managers may decline to address a problem with the performance or conduct of a particular employee. These are:

- The manager hopes that the problem might go away by itself, but of course it very rarely does, and instead will usually get worse;

- Lack of time, which although understandable, is not a valid excuse for not attending to one of the manager's most important responsibilities;

- Discomfort with the role of disciplinarian;

- A fear that if the problem is highlighted, more problems might crawl out of the woodwork;

- A fear of confrontation;

- Worry that working relationships might be damaged.

All of these are understandable responses, but they should not be allowed to get in the way of the effective and fair management of people problems.

The Importance of Tackling a Problem Promptly

It is very important for a manager to tackle any problem associated with an employee's conduct or performance promptly, i.e. as soon as the matter comes to the manager's attention. Otherwise:

- The employee is likely to assume that their performance or conduct (as the case may be) is acceptable;

- The problem behaviour will become a habit, and habits can be hard to break;

- Other staff may become de-motivated and possibly resentful, especially if they are expected to carry a colleague's work or suffer the consequences of their mistakes or lack of effort;

- A precedent may be set which others may then follow;

- The manager's credibility is likely to be severely damaged.

HOW TO IDENTIFY PROBLEMS

Managers should constantly be alert to the possibility of people problems arising. Some problems will be obvious, for example if an employee persistently arrives at work late. Other problems, such as a personality clash between two employees may not immediately be visible to the manager. Nevertheless, a manager who engages in regular effective face-to-face communication with staff and who is observant will soon notice that something is wrong, enabling the matter to be raised with a view to finding a solution. Problems can be identified in a number of ways, for example through:

- Ongoing general observation of employees' work methods and behaviour;

- Spot-checking on employees' work output;

- Consulting employees regularly (at informal meetings) about the issues and/or problems that affect them or that might be causing concern;

- Encouraging employees to give the manager feedback about the job, how it could be done better, what problems get in the way of effective performance and how such problems might be resolved;

- Asking customers or clients for feedback;

- Periodic appraisal reviews, whether formal or informal;

- Walking the job.

One way for a manager to engage with staff and increase the chances that any problem areas are noticed is for the manager regularly to "walk the job". This means simply walking around the part of the workplace where the employees are performing their work and talking to individuals informally about general matters. It is likely that the manager who does this regularly will be perceived as approachable and employees are therefore more likely to raise issues and share problems as and when they arise. In contrast, the manager who sits in an office all day and tells employees that their "door is always open" may well find that no employees ever come forward to disclose any worries or problems that they may have. This may be because:

- They think that the manager will not have time or will not be interested in their problem or query;

- They feel embarrassed at the prospect of being seen by their colleagues to knock on the manager's door;

- They fear criticism or rejection from the manager;

- They are shy, nervous, or too much in awe of the manager's senior position to volunteer an issue;

- They do not believe that they will be taken seriously.

The "my door is always open" approach is rarely effective on its own, but if the manager makes the effort to instigate informal talks with employees on a regular basis, and if they use their eyes and ears when doing so, then it is much more likely that they will pick up on any problem areas before they have had the opportunity to escalate into major issues.

Managers should avoid the obvious pitfall of assuming that there are no problems in their department just because no one has complained. As soon as a potential problem is noticed, action should be taken to investigate it and establish what can be done to improve or solve the matter.

Exploring the Cause(s) of the Problem

Once a problem has come to the manager's attention (by whatever means), the first task for the manager will be to explore its root cause. The manager should be careful not to make assumptions or jump to premature conclusions about employees' motives, the reasons for any unsatisfactory conduct or performance or about who is to blame for a particular problem. Instead the manager should maintain an open mind and investigate the matter objectively. This topic is explored further in the various chapters that follow in relation to specific issues.

EFFECTIVE PERFORMANCE MANAGEMENT –
GENERAL PRINCIPLES

One key factor in the effective management of staff is to ensure that employees who perform or behave well or badly (as the case may be) experience the appropriate consequences. In other words, managers should ensure that:

- "Good" behaviour is followed by positive consequences, for example praise or possibly some extra time off work.

- Extra work is not piled on to those who perform well – the employees concerned will soon learn that the "reward" for good performance or timely presentation of work is to be allocated even more responsibility or extra work.

- "Bad" behaviour or poor performance is not inadvertently followed up with positive consequences, for example less work is assigned to the employee in the future.

- Employees whose performance is below average in terms of quality of work or speed of output are not allowed to get away with doing less than their share of the work. The manager should instead commence performance management proceedings (see chapter 5).

Standard Setting Meetings

A "standard setting meeting" is an informal meeting between a manager and an employee, held in private, to discuss some aspect of the employee's conduct or performance that the manager views as unsatisfactory. Such a meeting will be the first step in managing the "problem" and should take place as soon as is reasonably practicable after the problem has come to the manager's attention.

It will be important, as stated earlier in this chapter, to tackle any instances of problem conduct, performance, attendance or behaviour promptly. Clearly this approach is suitable only for relatively minor problems that are in their early stages.

A standard setting meeting should have a structure along the following lines:

Introduction

Set the tone, format and scene – informal, friendly, confidential, supportive;

State the purpose of the interview, for example to discuss the employee's timekeeping, work output, etc;

Reassure the employee that the manager has a positive aim in mind, for example performance improvement or a desire to improve working relationships.

Define the problem

Raise the issue(s) – the manager should explain the problem to the employee, and state why it is a problem;

Give specific examples and avoid generalisations;

Keep the tone friendly, not accusatory;

Seek agreement from the employee that there is a problem and on the nature of the problem.

Get agreement as to the solution

Seek suggestions from the employee as to the improvement or action required;

Offer suggestions, if necessary, if the employee is unable to come up with the course of action needed to tackle the problem;

Offer support as appropriate;

Agree a timescale for improvement.

Explore alternatives

Allow the employee to suggest alternatives;

Discuss how these might resolve the problem;

Seek compromises where appropriate.

Commitment
Encourage the employee to summarise the action they will take;

Clarify any relevant standards, for example work standards;

Ensure the employee is committed to change.

Conclusion

Summarise what has been accomplished;

Summarise what has been agreed;

Let the employee know how/when the manager will follow up.

Giving Effective Feedback

Effective managers will deliver both genuine praise and constructive criticism to individual employees whenever the situation demands it. In order to be effective, the feedback should be delivered in accordance with the following general guidelines. The manager should:

- Give feedback promptly after the event to which it relates. The manager should *never* store up problems to raise with the employee at an annual appraisal interview.

- Do not be tempted to dig up past ills – if the matter was not important enough to be discussed at the time it occurred, it is neither fair nor constructive to raise it weeks or even months later.

- Deliver criticism in private and never in any circumstances in front of others.

- Check before delivering criticism that the problem under review is something over which the employee has control.

- Make feedback clear and specific, and not vague and woolly. Give specific examples of whatever the problem is.

- Avoid generalisations, for example "you're always late". Such generalisations are unlikely to be true or fair. Instead give the employee specific facts, for example "you have been late on three occasions in the last two weeks, each time between 15 and 30 minutes.

- Deliver feedback objectively and unemotionally, ensuring the tone of voice does not indicate annoyance or disapproval.

- Make feedback positive, not negative, i.e. make sure the employee understands what they have done wrong, why it is wrong, and what they are expected to do differently in the future.

- Never follow up praise with a "but" phrase. The word "but" often has the effect of negating what has just been said, for example "This is a good report, but the information in section three is out of date". Try substituting the word "and" and turning the sentence around to "This is a good report and once the information in section three has been brought up to date ....".

- Check for understanding following the delivery of criticism in order to make sure that what has been said has been fully and clearly understood. Receiving criticism is difficult for most people, and there is therefore a higher than average chance of misunderstandings arising. The manager should not be shy of repeating the key messages as repetition may help the employee to understand fully the implications of what has happened and what needs to be done to put matters right.

- Ensure criticism is constructive – see below.

There are two key factors that will make criticism constructive rather than destructive. These are to:

- Concentrate on the employee's actions or behaviour, and not on their personality;

- Concentrate on the future and not the past.

These principles are expanded on below:

Concentrating on actions and behaviour, not on personality traits

The manager should stick to facts when delivering criticism and avoid attacking the employee on a personal level. For example it will not be helpful to say "You're very careless" but much better instead to state "There are several mistakes in your work that I need to discuss with you". It will not be constructive to say "You have a bad attitude" but much more helpful to say "I noticed at the meeting yesterday that you disagreed with every proposal that was suggested ..."

Thus the manager should concentrate on what the employee has *done,* not on what they *are,* and refrain from delivering personal criticism or put-downs. It is decidedly unhelpful to give an employee a negative label, and much more effective for the manager to describe in factual terms what they have observed. This approach is also far less likely to cause an argument – after all an employee can hardly disagree with specific, proven facts.

It is important also to keep emotion out of any discussion about an employee's conduct or performance. No matter how angry, impatient or frustrated the manager might be feeling about what the employee has done (or not done, as the case may be), they should act rationally, objectively and fairly. Otherwise the manager will risk being perceived as unfair, irrational or possibly aggressive.

Concentrating on the future and not the past

The manager should take care, when giving criticism, to adopt a corrective approach and not a punitive, blaming one. There is no point harping on about what happened and how awful it is. Once the facts have been presented and discussed, it will be important to move on quickly to establish through discussion and agreement what can be done to put matters right, or to identify how the employee can avoid making the same mistake again. The manager should work together with the employee to identify an appropriate solution to the particular problem. Whilst it will, of course, be very important for the manager to make sure that the employee understands clearly what needs to be done to achieve improvement, it is equally important to communicate to the employee that the manager is on their side.

Although allocating blame is never constructive, it will be important for the manager to encourage the employee to take responsibility for their actions. In order to achieve this, it may be helpful to explain to the employee how their actions or behaviour affected others. Thus the manager may state clearly and in specific, observable and behavioural terms precisely what the person has done/not done, and the effect it had on them, the employee's colleagues, a customer or the organisation as a whole. For example, the manager might say "Because your work was presented three days late, that meant the customer had to wait for their report and their project leader has now written a letter of complaint to our general manager".

In explaining the consequences of actions or behaviour to an employee, the manager should of course take care not to cause undue or disproportionate distress. For example, it may not be helpful to tell an inexperienced employee who has made a genuine mistake that the company has lost a major contract as a result. The manager should therefore use judgement as to whether, and to what extent, to explain to the employee what the effects of their particular conduct or work output were.

Generally, the manager should be willing to support their employees in every aspect of their employment. Thus, when something has gone wrong, it is important that the employee is not made to feel like a victim, or subjected to some form of punishment. The employee needs to learn from the experience in order to reduce the probability of a reoccurrence.

Giving praise

Giving sincere praise is one of the simplest and most effective methods of motivating employees and encouraging good performance. Without occasional praise (where it is deserved) an employee is likely eventually to feel that they are wasting their time putting in effort and hard work. After all, why should they bother, if no one ever notices?

People at work need to feel that they are achieving something worthwhile, that their contributions matter, and that their skills and efforts are recognised and valued. Praise can achieve this, provided it is given plainly and sincerely.

Dealing with Emotional Reactions

Many managers, understandably, find it difficult to deliver criticism or even to discuss a workplace problem for fear that the employee may react emotionally. An emotional reaction may take a variety of different forms, such as:

- Silence, shock or disbelief;

- Crying;

- Anger or outrage;

- Indignation;

- Guilt or regret.

Although such emotional reactions may be difficult for the manager to deal with, it is important that the reaction is acknowledged, and not ignored or dismissed as inappropriate.

Here are some brief guidelines for dealing with emotional reactions:

- Listen to what the employee is saying, including the emotional reaction – allowing them to "let off steam" (within reason) may be helpful.

- Acknowledge the reaction by saying something simple such as "I can see you are upset about this".

- Within reason, communicate to the employee that is it OK to be upset, angry, etc, for example by saying "I can understand why you find this difficult".

- Do *not* contradict the employee at this stage – this only creates conflict. If they have said something that is inaccurate, this can be dealt with and, if necessary, put right, a little later once they have calmed down.

- Ask questions of the employee where appropriate. Questions show that the manager is taking the employee's reaction seriously. For example, the manager might ask: "what is the most important aspect of this situation from your point of view?"

- To defuse anger, try to find something in what the employee is saying that the manager can openly agree with, for example "yes, I agree that the situation is most unfortunate and should not have arisen".

- Empathise where appropriate, i.e. the manager should say something that shows the employee they understand their reaction, for example "we all make mistakes sometimes, let's focus on how to prevent a similar mistake occurring in the future".

- Do *not* act defensively if the employee retaliates in some way against the manager - defensiveness achieves nothing and may make matters worse. Instead remind the employee of what the discussion is about, if necessary.

- Be friendly in tone and manner, but also firm where necessary.

- Give reassurance to the employee where possible, in particular to reassure them that the manager is on their side.

- Focus on what can be done to solve the problem, rather than focussing on how awful things are.

- Try not to take the employee's reaction personally.

KEY POINTS

The manager should:

- Recognise that there are many different types of "people problems" that managers may have to deal with.

- Always tackle any problem associated with an employee's conduct or performance promptly as soon as it has come to the manager's attention.

- Engage in regular effective face-to-face communication with staff and be alert to the possibility of people problems arising.

- "Walk the job", i.e. talk to employees informally at their workstations rather than just telling employees that their "door is always open".

- Avoid assuming that there are no problems in the department just because no one has complained.

- Resist the temptation to allocate any extra work only to employees who perform well and allow those whose performance is below average to get away with doing less than their share.

- Conduct an informal standard setting meeting with an employee whenever some aspect of the employee's conduct or performance is unsatisfactory and needs to be discussed.

- Give both genuine praise and constructive criticism to individual employees whenever the situation demands it.

- Deliver criticism in private and never in any circumstances in front of others.

- Make feedback clear, give specific examples to the employee of whatever the problem is, and avoid generalisations.

- When delivering criticism, concentrate on the employee's actions or behaviour and not on their personality, and concentrate on the future, not the past.

CHAPTER 2
DEALING WITH DAY-TO-DAY
MISCONDUCT

INTRODUCTION

The term "misconduct" can cover many different forms of inappropriate, unsatisfactory or negative behaviour in the workplace.

This chapter, together with chapters 3 ("Dealing with Different Types of Misconduct") and 4 ("Dealing with Serious Misconduct Both in and out of Work"), deals with the subject of how managers should tackle employee misconduct. This chapter deals with day-to-day matters that may arise, ranging from very minor to moderately serious. Chapter 3 addresses some specific and often difficult types of misconduct, whilst chapter 4 deals with serious misconduct, including what to do where misconduct is suspected but not proven, and the appropriate course of action if an employee commits an act of misconduct, or even a crime, outside of work.

It is recommended that managers should familiarise themselves with the advice and guidance given in the ACAS Code of Practice on Disciplinary and Grievance Procedures, updated and republished in October 2004. Although the ACAS Code of Practice is not legally binding on employers, a failure to follow its recommendations will be taken into account by an employment tribunal if the employer is facing a claim for unfair dismissal. This means in effect that if the provisions of the Code have not been followed, the tribunal may decide that the employer has acted unreasonably, in which the case the employer is more likely to fail in their defence of the claim.

WHAT CONSTITUTES MISCONDUCT?

Misconduct at work may occur in many forms and is, ultimately, a potentially fair reason for dismissal in circumstances where an employee's misconduct continues following a series of warnings, or where further offences are committed. There is no definition in law as to what constitutes misconduct and no legal list of the types of behaviour that may be regarded in this light. Clearly every employer's business needs are different, and a particular type of behaviour may be acceptable to one employer whilst proving unacceptable to another. For example, it is normal practice in the oil industry to impose a complete ban on alcohol on offshore installations (including during rest periods), but may be equally normal in the London financial sector for employees to enjoy a drink or two at lunchtimes.

It is therefore up to each organisation to determine its own policies and rules on matters such as:

● Health and safety;

● Time-keeping;

● A requirement to work reasonable overtime when asked to do so;

● The prohibition of any form of discrimination or harassment;

● The duty to obey reasonable instructions;

● Care in handling money and company property;

● Use of company resources for example equipment, materials and stationery;

● Use of computer facilities, in particular use of e-mail and access to the internet.

Whatever the employer's rules are, it is essential that they are clearly and coherently written down and reliably communicated to every employee. Any changes to the rules should be vigorously drawn to employees' attention.

Some acts of misconduct will amount to gross misconduct justifying immediate dismissal of the employee without notice or pay in lieu of notice (termed "summary dismissal"). Gross misconduct and summary dismissal are covered in chapter 4. In other less serious cases, disciplinary sanctions other than dismissal will be appropriate, the most usual being the issuing of a verbal or written warning.

Cases of misconduct should always be dealt with exactly in accordance with the employer's own disciplinary procedure. Dismissal for a first offence would be appropriate only where the employee's misconduct was of a very serious nature, amounting to gross misconduct.

Whilst it would be impossible to list all the possible types of behaviour which might be viewed as misconduct, later sections in this chapter aim to address the most common conduct problems which managers may have to deal with.

As a starting point, managers should:

- Make sure they are familiar with and fully understand their organisation's disciplinary rules and procedures;

- Ensure that the rules, any changes to the rules, and the penalties applicable to breaches of the rules are properly communicated to all staff, not only at induction, but throughout employment;

- Make sure their staff properly understand the rules and the penalties applicable to any breaches of the rules;

- Ensure that rules and procedures are applied and enforced consistently, i.e. that no particular individual or group of employees is treated more strictly than others.

As regards the issue of consistency, it is well established that a dismissal for a particular type of misconduct is likely to be unfair if the employer has not in the past dismissed employees for similar offences. If, however, there are material differences between one situation and another, there may be justification for deciding to dismiss an employee even though another employee was not dismissed for committing the same type of offence.

An example of this type of allegedly inconsistent treatment arose in *Enterprise Liverpool plc v Bauress and Ealey EAT [2006] 0645/05*. Two employees, both joiners who had recently completed their apprenticeships, were provided by their employer with a van and tools in order to carry out repairs at the company's customers' premises. When it was established that they had used the van and materials to moonlight during working hours, both were dismissed. They brought claims of unfair dismissal to an employment tribunal – which were ultimately appealed through to the Employment Appeal Tribunal (EAT). One of the key features of the claim was an allegation that another employee who had previously committed the same offence had not been dismissed, but had been given a final written warning instead. This, the dismissed employees claimed, was evidence of inconsistent treatment sufficient to make their dismissals unfair.

The EAT found from the evidence presented by the employer that there were two clear differences between the circumstances of the previous employee and the two employees in the present case. Firstly, the previous employee, at the time of his misdemeanour, had 30 years service and a good record, whereas the two employees in this case were relatively recently out of their apprenticeships, each having only three years service. Secondly, the previous employee had, when challenged, admitted his guilt and been remorseful, whereas the two joiners had attempted to cover up their misconduct and had not shown any remorse.

The EAT held that it was within the band of reasonable responses for the employer to regard length of service and admission of guilt as distinguishing features when deciding to dismiss the two relatively junior employees. The dismissals were therefore fair.

This case demonstrates that, although consistency of treatment is the general rule, it can happen that there are material differences between the circumstances of an employee's misconduct in one case and the circumstances of a previous case, and that such circumstances may provide justification for different treatment.

It would be strongly advisable for any manager deciding to impose a penalty that is more severe (or less severe) than a penalty previously imposed on another employee for a similar offence to keep a written record of the specific reasons justifying the different treatment.

It is also advisable for managers to consult and involve their human resources department (if they have one) in all disciplinary matters, other than the sorts of very minor day-to-day issues that can be resolved through informal discussions.

DISCIPLINARY RULES AND PROCEDURES

Many managers, understandably, feel anxious about applying disciplinary rules and procedures. As discussed in chapter 1, they may fear confrontation, or worry that working relationships might be damaged if they speak to an employee about behaviour that they view as inappropriate or unacceptable. It may be that the particular matter is minor, and the manager takes the view that it is easier – at least in the short term – to let the matter go and say nothing about it. Doing nothing, however, rarely produces a satisfactory outcome as the employee whose conduct is in some way unsatisfactory is likely to assume that what they are doing (or not doing) is in fact acceptable since the manager has not said anything to indicate the contrary. Matters may well then escalate if the employee's misconduct is repeated.

The Purpose of Rules and Procedures

A constructive approach towards disciplinary rules and procedures would be to view the processes in the following light:

- Disciplinary rules set standards, and make it clear to all employees what conduct is and is not acceptable – this helps to prevent misunderstandings;

- Disciplinary procedures permit managers to deal fairly and consistently with employees who breach the rules, rather than dealing with someone in a random or unstructured fashion;

- Disciplinary procedures are not there for the purpose of punishing employees for wrongdoing, but rather as a process aimed at encouraging employees whose conduct is in some way unsatisfactory to improve.

The Stages of a Disciplinary Procedure

Most employers' formal disciplinary procedures are structured around a hierarchy of stages, with each stage having a defined

29

outcome (for example a warning). A typical procedure might look like this:

Stage 1:   Formal verbal warning

Stage 2:   Written warning

Stage 3:   Final written warning

Stage 4:   Dismissal with notice.

Further details of each of the above stages appear below.

There is no legal requirement that the procedure should have any defined number of stages, although ACAS (Advisory, Conciliatory and Arbitration Service) recommends that a procedure should allow for at least two warnings prior to dismissal.

Contrary to logic, there is no requirement always to enter the procedure at the beginning (although this would be appropriate for first instances of minor misconduct). What is important is to ensure that the type of penalty imposed is proportionate to the severity of the employee's offence.

For example, in *Stanley Cole (Wainfleet) Ltd v Sheridan [2003] IRLR 52,* the EAT held that a final written warning issued to an employee with five years unblemished service for a first offence that was relatively minor represented a breach of trust and confidence, and hence a fundamental breach of contract, entitling the employee to resign and claim constructive dismissal. The conduct giving rise to the final written warning was that the employee had, following a heated argument with a colleague which had upset her, taken an extra hour off work at lunchtime without permission. The EAT held that the penalty of a final written warning in these circumstances was disproportionate and unjustified.

In contrast, it may well be appropriate to give an employee a final written warning for an instance of serious misconduct that is a first offence if the nature of the misconduct is severe enough to justify this level of penalty. Examples may include breaches of safety rules or other conduct that falls short of gross misconduct but which is nevertheless very serious.

Informal Discussions about Unsatisfactory Conduct

Not all forms of misconduct will give rise to the need to follow formal procedures. In many instances, it will be appropriate for the manager to sit down informally with the employee to discuss the behaviour that has given cause for concern. This approach would be appropriate in the event of a first or minor offence or a series of incidents which, when considered together, could represent the beginning of problem conduct.

To pursue this course of action, the manager should:

- Hold an informal meeting in private with the employee to make them aware of the conduct that is viewed as inappropriate or unsatisfactory.

- Explain how and why the particular conduct is causing a problem. The phrase "I have noticed that ..." is useful, e.g. "I have noticed that sometimes you raise your voice when you speak to other staff ..." or "I have noticed that you often spend long periods of time chatting on the telephone".

- Give specific examples if possible, such as "last Thursday when you shouted at John about the monthly report being late, he was really upset afterwards" or "yesterday you were on the phone to Jane for over half an hour".

- Be factual and not judgemental.

- Ask the employee to explain the reason(s) for the conduct in question.

- Be prepared to listen to what the employee is saying.

- Explain in a factual way how the behaviour affects other people, for example, "Jenny, when you miss the deadline for your monthly report, then the result is that others are unable to complete their work on time".

- Explain clearly what change in the employee's behaviour is necessary or what specific action is required, for example "why don't you start work on the report two days earlier each month and, if by chance you don't have all the information you need by that time, come and see me".

- Seek cooperation and agreement on how to ensure that the problem conduct does not continue or recur.

- Try to finish the discussion on a positive note, for example by reassuring the employee of the manager's desire to maintain or improve working relationships, or by reminding them that their skills or experience in the job are valued.

- Set a date to review the employee's conduct again.

Although such a meeting is informal (and would therefore not attract the right to be accompanied – see below), the manager should keep a record of the meeting. The record would show simply:

- The date and time of the meeting;

- The matter under discussion, for example lateness;

- The fact that there was no formal outcome;

- When the employee's conduct will be reviewed again.

It is as well to give the employee a copy of the file note since they would have the right of access to it in any event under the subject access provisions of the *Data Protection Act 1998* (which covers most manual files as well as computer-based records).

FAIR PROCEDURE – AN OVERVIEW

There are a number of procedural issues to be addressed prior to, and after, taking a decision as to whether to impose formal disciplinary action against an employee. When dealing with misconduct, the manager should:

- Investigate the issue thoroughly before setting up a disciplinary interview with the employee.

- Give the employee adequate written details of the case against them in advance of the interview, including copies of any witness statements.

- Set up a disciplinary interview, giving the employee reasonable notice and telling them that the interview is to be held under the organisation's disciplinary procedure.

- Inform the employee that they have the right, if they wish, to bring a "companion" to the interview (see below under "The Right to be Accompanied at a Disciplinary Interview").

- At the interview, put all the relevant facts to the employee, for example if the problem concerns repeated mistakes in the employee's work, the employee should be shown examples.

- Give the employee a full and fair hearing, i.e. a proper opportunity to challenge the evidence against them, explain their conduct and put forward any mitigating factors.

- Consider carefully any mitigating factors or explanations put forward by the employee and, where appropriate, be prepared to show support and understanding.

- Adjourn to decide on the appropriate course of action.

- Communicate the outcome - first verbally, and subsequently in writing.

- Include a clear statement in any warning issued of what the consequences will be for the employee if there are further instances of misconduct.

- Allow a right of appeal if the decision is to issue a formal warning.

- Act objectively and reasonably in an overall sense throughout the process.

- Keep a written record of the interview – there is no need to record everything that was said (although this may be advisable in particularly difficult cases) but all the main points under discussion should be recorded and a copy given to the employee.

All disciplinary interviews should, of course, be held in private, and the employee being interviewed has the right to be treated with courtesy and respect, irrespective of what they are alleged to have done. The above matters are explored further below.

THE IMPORTANCE OF GETTING THE FACTS RIGHT BEFORE TAKING ACTION

Managers should avoid acting hastily or reacting in anger to an employee's misconduct. Instead they should approach the matter objectively and deal with it one step at a time. Equally, the manager should not, when an employee's alleged misconduct comes to their attention, jump to instant conclusions but should instead investigate the matter properly and with an open mind in order to ensure fairness.

It is understandable, when faced with apparent inappropriate conduct on the part of an employee, for a manager to feel angry, frustrated or impatient with the employee. It is, however, very important not to allow these emotions to get in the way of fair and objective handling of the matter. Instead, the manager should embark on a process of investigation to establish the facts, before rushing into formal disciplinary action. After all, without a proper investigation, the manager will not be able to have a structured or constructive discussion with the employee about whatever the employee is supposed to have done wrong.

An example of a manager who jumped to negative conclusions about an employee's conduct without proper grounds was put before an employment tribunal in the case of Sovereign Business Integration plc v Trybus [2007] EAT 0107/07. Mr Trybus worked as a senior sales executive before he was summarily dismissed on account of his employer's contention that he had been absent without authority on a particular day - it was alleged that he had not made the visits to clients that were recorded in his diary - and on grounds of possible improper use of electronic communications.

Prior to his dismissal, Mr Trybus had raised concerns on several occasions about the calculation of his commission and the distribution of work. Shortly after he indicated that he wished these matters to be treated as a formal grievance, he was suspended, pending an investigation into his alleged unauthorised absence.

Subsequently, the manager sent Mr Trybus a copy of an "investigation report" that she had compiled and a disciplinary hearing was arranged. The day before the hearing was due to take place, Mr Trybus sent in a doctor's certificate for four weeks, citing "work-related stress". Convinced that this was a delaying tactic, the manager said she would only delay the hearing until 5.00 pm that evening to allow Mr Trybus time to reply to a number of questions. As the manager did not receive a response, the hearing went ahead and the decision to dismiss was taken.

The tribunal found that the dismissal was unfair because the company's investigation into the alleged misconduct was completely one-sided and was not carried out with an open mind. This, said the tribunal, "coloured the whole of the investigation and the treatment of the claimant thereafter". No attempt had been made to contact clients to ask whether Mr Trybus had visited them, and he had not been given the opportunity to put his side of the story in full. The tribunal also found from the evidence that the manager had resented the claimant's persistence in raising grievances over his commission and work distribution.

The tribunal also said that the manager had acted completely unreasonably in failing to delay the disciplinary hearing. Although the manager believed the absence was not genuine, there was no evidence to back up that belief. The tribunal's decision was upheld on appeal to the EAT who judged that the employer's failure to contact witnesses or obtain Mr Trybus's answers to questions rendered its investigation inadequate and the dismissal unfair. This was all the more so because the employer had been prejudiced against Mr Trybus from the start.

In investigating an employee's alleged misconduct, the manager should:

- Examine any relevant written records, for example previous disciplinary warnings, appraisal reports, managers' notes, etc.

- Consult other managers with whom the employee has come into contact (if appropriate) in order to help establish relevant facts.

- Seek written statements from any employees who may have been witness to the employee's alleged misconduct (see chapter

4 for more detailed information on witnesses and witness' statements).

- Assess whether or not the employee's conduct is worse than the standard that is generally required of employees. For example in a case of absenteeism, seek advice from human resources department if possible as to what is a "normal" level and/or frequency of absence within the organisation as a whole.

- Conduct an investigatory interview with the employee if appropriate, making sure the employee knows that the purpose of the interview is to establish the facts and that the interview is not part of the disciplinary procedure.

- Take an objective and balanced view of any information that comes to light, and avoid allowing personal views, opinions, likes or dislikes to influence the assessment of the employee's conduct.

Some employers operate an investigation procedure alongside their disciplinary procedure with the former preceding the latter. The purpose of a separate investigation procedure is to establish the facts before a decision is taken as to whether there are proper grounds for the manager to invoke the disciplinary procedure. Where the employer does operate two separate procedures, the manager who conducts the investigation should not be the same person who subsequently implements the disciplinary procedure.

There is no requirement in law to operate separate investigation and disciplinary procedures. Many larger organisations with different layers of management may find it helpful to do so, whilst smaller organisations may find it unnecessarily time-consuming or even confusing to have to work with two procedures.

INFORMING THE EMPLOYEE OF THE ALLEGED MISCONDUCT

It is important that any employee accused of misconduct is given all the facts about their alleged wrongdoing in advance of any disciplinary interview. There are good reasons for this, in particular to ensure that natural justice is served. A disciplinary interview, to be fair, must be set up in such a way that the employee is given the opportunity to prepare for it. An interview convened on the spur of the moment, or one arranged without the employee first being fully informed of the issues to be discussed is unlikely to provide an environment conducive to the achievement of natural justice.

In the event that the employee is dismissed following the interview, such an approach is also likely to lead an employment tribunal to conclude that the employer acted unreasonably and that the dismissal was therefore unfair.

The manager should therefore make sure that the employee is informed in writing in advance of the interview what the basis is for the manager believing that there may be grounds for disciplinary action, i.e. the manager should give adequate information to the employee without giving the appearance that they have already made up their mind what the outcome will be. Vague, woolly statements such as "management have some problems with the way you are doing your job" will clearly be insufficient. Instead the information provided to the employee should be specific enough to allow the employee to prepare properly for the disciplinary interview.

Notice to come to a Disciplinary Interview

In setting up a disciplinary interview, the manager should give the employee reasonable notice, inform them that the interview will be held under the banner of the organisation's disciplinary procedure and state that the outcome could be disciplinary action or dismissal, as appropriate.

There is no recommended or minimum time-scale for such notice laid down in statute, but the key objective is to allow the employee enough time to think about the issues that are to be discussed and prepare a response. A day or so may be enough for a straightforward issue such as persistent lateness, whilst a week's notice or even longer may be required if the employee is accused of serious misconduct (in which case the employee would normally be suspended with pay until after the interview).

The Right to be Accompanied at a Disciplinary Interview

The law allows all employees to choose to be accompanied at any formal disciplinary interview (or formal grievance hearing). The basic statutory provisions are that:

- All employees have the right in law to bring a "companion" to a formal disciplinary or grievance hearing if they wish;

- The companion may be a fellow worker or an accredited trade union official;

- The companion must be someone whom the employee (not the manager) has selected - even if the manager considers that the employee's choice of companion is inappropriate, they have no say in the matter;

- The companion (if a fellow-worker) must be granted paid time off work.

It is important to note that, if an employee wishes to bring a trade union official to a disciplinary interview as their companion, the manager must accede to this request irrespective of whether the trade union is one recognised by the employer. Furthermore, the trade union official does not have to be an employee of the same organisation. Employees have no right (unless their contract of employment states otherwise) to bring any other outsider to the interview, for example a solicitor or relative. The matter is an internal one, and the involvement of an outsider is usually inadvisable as it may complicate the processes. There may be a valid exception in the case of a very young employee who may benefit from the opportunity to be accompanied by a parent or close friend or an employee with learning difficulties who should normally be permitted to bring along a supportive person of their choice.

The role of the companion

It is provided in law that the companion may:

- Address the hearing on behalf of the employee, i.e. put the employee's case (if the employee so wishes);

- Confer with the employee during the hearing;

- Sum up the employee's case;

- Respond on the employee's behalf to any views expressed at the hearing.

The interviewer is entitled, however, to expect the employee (and not the companion) to answer any questions asked.

Postponing the interview

If the employee's chosen companion is not available to attend a meeting at the time nominated by the employer, the employee has the right to request a postponement of up to five working days. Such a postponement need only be granted once. Furthermore, the delay must be reasonable when considering the needs of the managers and any witnesses who are to attend the interview. In the event that the chosen companion is away on a work assignment or on holiday, then the employee should be asked to choose another companion who is available and who would not have to travel a long distance to attend the interview.

Who should attend from the management side?

Although there is no law that dictates who should attend or conduct a disciplinary interview from the management side, it is advisable for the manager who is conducting the interview to arrange for another member of management or (even better) an HR representative to be present. This is a safeguard in case the employee should become aggressive or make false or malicious allegations later on about how the interview was conducted. The second member of management can also fill the role of note-taker, so that an accurate record of the interview can be made.

Dealing with an Employee who "Throws A Sickie"

It can happen, once an employer has written to an employee informing them that a disciplinary interview is to be convened to discuss an allegation of misconduct, that the employee soon afterwards informs the employer that they are ill and unable to attend work. This may of course be absolutely genuine, or alternatively may be a ruse on the employee's part to avoid "facing the music". A medical certificate stating "stress", "anxiety" or depression" may well follow.

Managers should never assume in these circumstances that the employee's absence is not genuine, unless there is clear evidence to this effect (see the *Trybus* case above).

Naturally it would be reasonable for the manager to postpone a disciplinary interview for a reasonable period of time to allow the employee to recover and return to work, and this is what managers should normally do. If, however, the employee's absence continues into several weeks or even months, a delay in dealing with the disciplinary matter may create new problems. There are often sound reasons for an employer to seek to resolve a disciplinary matter sooner rather than later, for example if the employee has been accused of bullying another employee, it might not be fair to the other employee to delay indefinitely. Arguably, it is in the absent employee's interests too to have the matter resolved sooner rather than later, as any stress or anxiety they are experiencing may well be exacerbated by the uncertainty and worry about what the outcome of the disciplinary process will be.

In this eventuality, the manager may wish to seek to obtain a medical assessment of the employee's fitness to attend a disciplinary interview, preferably from an occupational doctor. Just because an employee is unfit to work, this does not necessarily mean they are unable to attend a meeting for an hour or so. If the employee is declared fit enough to attend a disciplinary meeting, but still refuses to do so, they will be acting in breach of the implied duty to cooperate and will thus be in breach of contract.

The manager may wish to suggest to the employee that the interview could be held at a location other than the workplace to reduce the difficulties the employee may otherwise experience, whether with travelling or the prospect of having to face colleagues in the workplace. Such alternative arrangements could be to hold the meeting at a neutral venue (for example in a private room in a hotel) or even at the employee's home, provided the employee is prepared to consent to this without pressure and is comfortable with the idea.

Naturally if a doctor states that the employee is not well enough to attend a disciplinary interview, then the manager should not press the employee into attending.

In that case, the manager has a number of options and should write to the employee to set these out. The options are to:

- Suggest to the employee that a telephone discussion might be held in lieu of a face-to-face interview; or

- Inform the employee fully in a letter of the allegations against them and invite them to make written submissions instead of attending an interview; and/or

- Invite the employee to nominate a representative to attend the interview in their place; or

- Decide on what disciplinary action to take without any input from the employee.

The last option – proceeding to a decision without any input from the employee or their representative should only be considered after all other options have been exhausted. Relevant factors that may be taken into account when determining whether to proceed to a decision without a discussion with the employee include:

- How long the employee has been absent;

- How much longer the absence is expected to last;

- How important it is that the matter is dealt with promptly;

- Whether any delay in dealing with the disciplinary matter is likely to have a detrimental effect on other employees;

- Whether the employee's conduct, whilst absent, has been consistent with their stated inability to attend a meeting.

HOW TO CONDUCT A DISCIPLINARY INTERVIEW FAIRLY

The procedure for conducting a disciplinary interview should include the following important points for the manager, who should:

- Prepare thoroughly.

- Hold the disciplinary interview in a private place without interruptions, ensuring that discussions are kept confidential. Disciplining an employee in front of others (even for a minor offence) is embarrassing for everyone present, degrading to the employee, and may lead to accusations of bullying or victimisation.

- Inform the employee clearly at the start that the purpose of the interview is to assess whether the employee's conduct might warrant disciplinary action in accordance with the company's disciplinary procedure.

- Give the employee a clear, specific and factual account of management's view of the alleged misconduct.

- Inform the employee of the full extent of the evidence against them (bearing in mind that the key facts should have been provided in writing prior to the interview).

- Tell the employee about the content of any witnesses' statements and ideally give the statements to the employee to read (if this has not already been done).

- If it is reasonable to do so, give the employee the chance to question any witnesses' directly about their evidence (see chapter 4 for further information on witnesses' statements).

- Focus on the employee's behaviour and not on their personality.

- Avoid blame, accusations and personal remarks.

- Keep the approach reasonably formal and polite.

- Avoid open argument with the employee, but instead give them a full opportunity to state their views.

- Use open questions to encourage the employee to talk openly about the problem.

- Listen actively to the employee's version of events, giving them a full and fair opportunity to respond and put forward any mitigating factors.

- Bear in mind that there may be factors that have contributed towards the situation of which the manager is unaware.

- If new information comes to light during the interview, or if the employee completely disputes the allegations, adjourn the interview in order to carry out further investigation (for example, to interview a new witness and/or consider matters further).

- Seek to reach agreement on the nature and extent of the problem, and why the employee's conduct constitutes a problem for the employer.

- If, through discussions with the employee, it is agreed that a change or improvement to conduct is necessary, discuss the level of improvement required and encourage the employee to agree to work positively towards improvement (see below).

- If it has been established that the employee is guilty of misconduct, make sure they understand clearly that if the misconduct in question is repeated, then further formal disciplinary action at the next stage of the procedure will be taken against them. This should be stated factually and not in a threatening manner, bearing in mind that improvement in an employee's conduct is a much better outcome for both parties than further disciplinary action.

- After discussions have run their full course, sum up the main points concerning management's view of the employee's conduct, the main points raised by the employee, and any matters that need to be investigated further.

- Adjourn in order to make a decision about whether to impose a disciplinary penalty and if so the level and type of penalty to impose. The employee's responses and any mitigating factors put forward should be taken into account in taking this decision.

- Keep a written record of the interview.

Setting Targets for Improvement

Apart from discussing the nature of the employee's misconduct and why it occurred, one of the key purposes of a disciplinary interview will be to establish what the employee needs to do to improve or change. The starting point for this is to reach the position where the employee:

- Acknowledges that their conduct has created a problem;

- Understands the nature and extent of the problem and why it is a problem;

- Accepts that a change is required.

The manager conducting the interview should define and discuss the type and level of improvement required. The manager should also actively encourage the employee to work towards improvement, and should ensure that they are offered any appropriate support to help them improve, for example on-the-job coaching, if the problem involves unsatisfactory work standards.

GIVING WARNINGS

As discussed above under "The Stages of a Procedure", employers' formal disciplinary procedures are usually structured around a hierarchy of stages, with the outcome of each stage (other than the last stage) being a formal warning.

Stage 1 – Formal Verbal Warning

In the event that an employee's conduct does not improve following an informal discussion about the matter, the manager may, following an interview with the employee, issue a formal verbal warning. This could also be the course of action for a first breach of discipline or unsatisfactory job performance which can reasonably be viewed as the employee's fault. Although the warning is given orally, a record of the fact the warning was given, and the details of the misconduct and the employee's explanations for it should be kept on file.

Stage 2 – First Written Warning

Where an employee has already received a formal verbal warning and where there has subsequently been a further incidence of misconduct (whether of the same or a different type), where there has been an accumulation of minor offences, or where a first instance of misconduct is of a relatively serious nature, the outcome might be a written warning. As with all stages of discipline, the warning should be given only after a full investigation of the facts has taken place, and the employee interviewed to establish their side of events (see above).

Stage 3 – Final Written Warning

A final written warning would normally follow on from the previous stages of the disciplinary procedure if there is a further instance of misconduct or a failure to change or improve following the previous warnings. A final written warning may also be given, following investigation and an interview with the employee, where an employee's first offence is serious enough to warrant it.

Dismissal Following a Series of Warnings

The final stage of the disciplinary procedure – dismissal – may be the outcome where the employee, following a series of warnings, repeats the misconduct or fails to change or improve to the standard set at the time of previous warnings. Such a dismissal is capable of being fair in law, provided the employer has followed all the necessary aspects of procedure and acted reasonably overall. When dismissing in these circumstances, the employer must give notice of dismissal (or pay in lieu of notice) according to the terms of the employee's contract (see chapter 8).

The Content of a Warning

Disciplinary warnings should state:

- The nature of the employee's misconduct and the reason for the manager's dissatisfaction;

- The improvement required, i.e. a clear indication of how the employee is expected to behave in the future;

- Any timescale for improvement;

- The period of time the warning will remain active, which, once stated, must be adhered to;

- The outcome if there is no improvement, if improvement is not sustained or if unsatisfactory conduct is repeated, i.e. further disciplinary action at the next level of the procedure;

- The right to appeal against the warning and the timescale for doing so.

These matters are covered in more detail below.

Even if the warning given is a formal verbal warning, it is sound practice to keep a record of the fact that a warning was given, the date it was given, an indication of the conduct giving rise to the warning and the key points discussed at the disciplinary interview.

Warnings for Different Types of Misconduct

It is advisable for the employer to structure all warning letters so that they make it clear to the employee that any further act of misconduct (whether similar in nature to the employee's earlier misconduct or not) will lead to further disciplinary action at the next stage of the procedure. If the wording of the warning is too narrow, it may be difficult for the manager to follow through the disciplinary procedure in the event of further misconduct of a different kind. The result could be that the manager has to go back to the first stage of the disciplinary procedure each time the employee commits a new and different act of misconduct. Thus warnings should therefore first identify the employee's specific misconduct, then state that further misconduct *of any kind* will lead to further disciplinary action at the next stage of the disciplinary procedure.

The Need for Improvement

The warning should state in unambiguous terms that if there is no improvement in the employee's conduct within a defined timescale (see below), or if the misconduct in question is repeated, then further formal disciplinary action will be taken, leading potentially to eventual dismissal. This type of statement is particularly important at the final written warning stage, i.e. the employee must be told unequivocally that dismissal will be the outcome of further misconduct or a failure to improve.

Timescale for Improvement

In stating the improvement required, the manager should also, where appropriate agree a reasonable timescale with the employee for the desired level of improvement to be achieved. In the case of misconduct such as unsatisfactory timekeeping, the timescale for improvement will normally be immediate, i.e. the requirement will be for the employee to come to work on time from now on. With other forms of misconduct, there may be a need for a reasonable period of time for the employee to improve their knowledge of (for example) safety matters, the employer's computer policy, etc.

The "Shelf-Life" of a Warning

Most employers adopt a policy whereby different types of warning have a "shelf-life", i.e. they are deemed to remain active on an employee's file for disciplinary purposes for a stated period of time. Typical time periods would be:

Formal verbal warning	6 months
First written warning	12 months
Final written warning	24 months

There is, however, no law that dictates these (or any other) time periods and each employer is entitled to determine its own policy on how long any disciplinary warning should remain active.

Managers should bear in mind that where an employee has been informed that a warning will elapse after a defined period of time, this must be adhered to. Where a warning has elapsed, the employer is no longer entitled to take it into account in determining what penalty to impose on an employee who commits a further act of misconduct. This principle is especially important in the case of a final written warning. For example, in *Diosynth Ltd v Thomson Court of Session [2006] IRLR 284,* the employee's dismissal was ruled unfair on account of the fact that the employer's decision to dismiss relied on a written warning for similar conduct which had expired some four months earlier. This was despite the fact that the employee had committed a very serious breach of safety procedures and admitted failing to follow the required procedures on three occasions and falsifying the records to conceal these failures.

There were two problems with the written warning. Firstly, it had not been a final written warning, and secondly, the employer was not entitled to rely on a warning that had expired. The Court held that an employee is entitled to have a reasonable expectation that their employer means what it says if it states that a warning will be disregarded after a fixed period of time.

The EAT has also stated in another case that that it may, in certain circumstances, be appropriate for an employer to issue a warning for a longer period than usual, for example where a final written warning is given in lieu of dismissal (i.e. where the employer has chosen to be lenient in circumstances where they could have dismissed the employee for gross misconduct). Care should be taken with this, however, as it might be necessary for an employer to make formal changes to procedures so as to provide this flexibility, i.e. so that the right is reserved to extend the duration of warnings in certain defined circumstances.

The fact that a warning has expired does not oblige the employer to physically destroy the warning letter (unless employees' contracts or the disciplinary procedure states that this will happen). It may be advisable to retain the warning on the employee's file so that the employee's complete disciplinary record is available to management for purposes other than discipline. Care should be taken, however, to ensure that such an approach is allowed for in the organisation's policy or disciplinary procedure.

Allowing a Right of Appeal

Most disciplinary procedures allow for the right of appeal against all formal disciplinary decisions and it is good practice to afford employees this right. In the case of a dismissal, the employee should always be granted the right of appeal.

In order to be fair, an appeal must be conducted by someone other than the person who took the decision to dismiss the employee or issue a warning. Even a manager who has in some way been involved in the disciplinary proceedings relating to the employee, for example as the person responsible for an investigation into the employee's conduct, is unlikely to be capable of acting without bias.

Ideally the manager conducting the appeal should be someone more senior than the person who conducted the disciplinary interview. In small organisations, where a decision to impose disciplinary action may have been taken by the most senior person in the organisation, this will clearly not be possible. In the event of an unfair dismissal claim, the employment tribunal will take genuine practical problems of this type into account in assessing the fairness of the employer's actions and will not penalise the employer for failing to do something which they simply could not do. The most important issue is that the employee is treated so far as is possible according to the principles of natural justice.

Following Up

Once the disciplinary process has been completed, the manager should not just forget about the matter. It will be important to review the employee's conduct again at the time that was previously agreed. A follow-up has several advantages:

- The employee knows that their conduct is being monitored and is therefore more likely to make an effort to improve.

- If the employee has improved, there is an opportunity for the manager to give positive feedback at the time of the review, and this in turn is likely to encourage the employee to sustain the improvement.

- In the event that the employee's conduct has not improved sufficiently (or at all), there is an opportunity for the manager to discuss the situation with the employee again and decide whether to extend the deadline for improvement, set new targets or alternatively invoke the disciplinary procedure again.

KEY POINTS

Managers should:

- Recognise that, since there is no legal definition as to what types of behaviour are to be regarded as misconduct, it is up to each employer to determine their own policies and rules on a variety of matters.

- Always deal with employee misconduct exactly in accordance with the employer's in-house disciplinary procedure.

- View disciplinary rules and procedures constructively, i.e. as a process aimed at encouraging employees whose conduct is unsatisfactory to improve.

- In the event of a first or minor offence, speak to the employee informally to discuss the behaviour that the manager views as inappropriate.

- Always investigate any incident of alleged misconduct thoroughly and with an open mind and refrain from jumping to quick conclusions.

- Make sure that any employee accused of misconduct is given all the facts about their alleged wrongdoing in advance of any disciplinary interview.

- Make sure that any employee invited to attend a formal disciplinary interview is informed of their right to bring a fellow worker or trade union official along with them.

- If an employee is off sick at the time a disciplinary interview is convened and remains off sick for a lengthy period, write to the employee about the disciplinary matter and set out various options as to how the matter might be progressed.

- At a disciplinary interview, give the employee a clear, specific and factual account of management's view of their alleged misconduct together with the full extent of the evidence against them, and listen actively to the employee's side of the story, giving the employee a full and fair opportunity to respond.

- Actively encourage an employee whose conduct has been unsatisfactory to work towards improvement, and ensure that the employee is offered any appropriate support to help them improve.

- Structure all warning letters so that they make it clear to the employee that any further act of misconduct (whether similar in nature to the employee's earlier misconduct or not) will lead to further disciplinary action at the next stage of the disciplinary procedure.

- Bear in mind that, where an employee has been informed that a warning will elapse after a defined period of time, this time period must be adhered to.

- Always grant an employee who is issued with a formal disciplinary warning, or who is dismissed, the right to appeal, if possible to a more senior person.

CHAPTER 3
DEALING WITH DIFFERENT TYPES OF MISCONDUCT

INTRODUCTION

This chapter aims to explore some specific types of misconduct and how managers should approach them. The detail of the steps to take and general guidelines are given in the previous chapter.

UNSATISFACTORY TIMEKEEPING

Generally one or two instances of lateness would give rise to an informal interview with the employee to establish the underlying cause and remind them that lateness is unacceptable. Ultimately, persistent lateness without good reason could result in the employee being fairly dismissed following appropriate warnings, but a much more satisfactory outcome would be for the employee's timekeeping to improve following supportive action on the manager's part. The manager should, of course, always explore thoroughly the reasons for an employee's lateness. Reasons could include genuine family problems such as a childminder turning up late or difficulties with an elderly dependent relative living at home with the employee.

Whilst it is undoubtedly an employee's personal responsibility to get to work on time, it may be nevertheless be appropriate for a manager to demonstrate a reasonable level of tolerance and support to an employee who has genuine difficulties that are outside their control. It is, for example, within an employee's control to leave home early enough to cope with potential traffic delays, but outside their control if their child has unexpectedly fallen sick that morning.

MISTAKES AND CARELESSNESS

Where an employee is making frequent mistakes in their work, or at least appears to the manager to be careless, then the manager should take great care to explore the cause of those mistakes or perceived -

carelessness. In particular it will be essential to investigate and speak to the employee in order to establish whether or not the recurrence of mistakes or apparent carelessness is due to factors that are within the employee's control. There are many potential causes of poor work standards (explored thoroughly in chapter 5) that may be caused or exacerbated by factors in the workplace. One simple example is an employee who has not received sufficient training in order to perform the work to a satisfactory standard – little wonder that such an employee would make mistakes.

Thus, any incidence of mistakes or apparent carelessness should be regarded as misconduct only where it is clear, following investigations, that the unsatisfactory work standards are not due to factors outside the employee's control.

DEALING WITH AN EMPLOYEE WHO HAS A "BAD ATTITUDE"

Poor attitude is one of the hardest matters for any manager to tackle, largely because the impression that an employee has a poor attitude will, inevitably, be based on personal perception, i.e. the manager's view of the employee's conduct will -understandably – be based on their own standards and expectations. Managers need to take great care not to make unwarranted assumptions about an employee's attitude. Instead, the manager should:

- Seek to identify specific examples of the employee's conduct that have caused the manager to form the view that the employee has a negative attitude, i.e. specific, detailed examples of things the employee has said, done or failed to do. Examples could include instances where the employee refused to listen to someone else's point of view at a meeting; spoke in an aggressive manner to a colleague; failed to follow a specific instruction for no good reason; or failed to cooperate with colleagues in carrying out a particular piece of work.

- Investigate these examples if possible to establish whether there may have been any underlying reasons or background factors affecting the employee's conduct at the time in question, for example the employee may have been working under extreme pressure at the time of a particular incident.

- View what the employee said or did objectively without allowing personal opinions or emotions to get in the way of reasoned judgement.

- Speak to the employee in order to put the established examples of perceived inappropriate conduct to them as matters of fact (rather than opinion). For example, avoid statements such as "you are sometimes aggressive when you speak to your colleagues" which is vague and opinion-based, and instead make a specific, factual statement such as "at the planning meeting last Tuesday you shouted at Tom in an aggressive manner when he commented on your proposal".

- Communicate to the employee that the purpose of the meeting is to discuss and resolve a problem, rather than criticise.

- Explain the consequences of the employee's conduct, for example another employee may have been upset by a particular incident.

- Ask the employee whether they are willing to accept that the behaviour in the specific examples raised represents inappropriate conduct (the employee may or may not accept this, but the question is worth asking anyway).

- Put to the employee that a change in behaviour is required, and if possible give specific examples of ways in which the employee might be expected to behave in future as alternatives to the ways in which they did behave in the various examples.

- Avoiding using terminology such as "bad attitude", as no employee is likely to accept that they have a bad attitude no matter what the circumstances are, and such a blanket accusation is likely to provoke an even more negative reaction on the part of the employee.

- Be supportive throughout the meeting, i.e. the manager should show the employee that they are on the employee's side.

The technique to deal with perceived poor attitude is therefore to establish facts (and not opinions), put these facts to the employee at a private meeting, give specific examples of incidences of inappropriate conduct, invite comment and seek to establish a change in the employee's behaviour. Clearly the sooner such instances of unacceptable behaviour are raised with the employee, the better.

BREACHES OF COMPANY POLICIES AND RULES

If an employer has in place clear policies and rules, then it will be relatively straightforward for a manager to identify any occasion on which an employee has acted in breach of a policy or rule.

Health and Safety Rules

Most managers would, rightly, view any breaches of their organisation's health and safety rules seriously. That is not to say, however, that every breach should be regarded as grounds for dismissal or even formal disciplinary action. The manager will need to investigate what happened and consider:

- Whether the employee's breach of a safety rule was deliberate (for example horse-play) or accidental (for example caused by a genuine mistake or oversight);

- Whether or not the breach of health and safety rules led, or could have led, to any serious consequence, for example someone being injured;

- Whether or not the employee has received adequate training in health and safety matters, and whether they were properly trained and experienced in the type of work they were performing at the time;

- Whether there were any mitigating factors, for example the employee may have been distracted by someone else at the time of a particular incident, or may not have been properly supervised;

- Whether the employee's conduct was a first instance of a safety breach or whether the employee has had previous warnings for similar offences.

The manager dealing with safety breaches should take a fair and objective approach, and should investigate the particular incident thoroughly before deciding whether to take disciplinary action against the employee.

Misuse of E-mail and the Internet

It is strongly advisable for employers to have clear written policies and rules for employees on use of e-mail and access to the internet through workplace computers. Such policies may also be usefully extended to include use of laptops, palm-tops and blackberries.

Problems that frequently arise include downloading sexually explicit material from the internet for employees' own amusement, spending an inordinate amount of time sending personal e-mails, using the internet for personal purposes during working time, and using inappropriate language (for example sexist or racist terminology) in internal e-mails which may cause offence to colleagues or others.

Managers should be constantly alert to the possibility of these and other potential abuses of e-mail and the internet. Even though a manager may think it is obvious that certain types of behaviour at work are inappropriate, they should not assume that all employees view such conduct in this way. For example, in *Dunn v IBM United Kingdom Ltd [1998] Case No 2305087/97,* the employee, who was dismissed following evidence that he had accessed and downloaded pornography and other non-business-related material from the internet, succeeded in a claim of unfair dismissal. This was largely because the employer had not communicated clearly to the employee that such activities would be likely to be regarded as gross misconduct leading to dismissal.

Smoking

Smoking is now banned throughout the UK in enclosed public places and workplaces with only very limited exceptions for some residential establishments such as care homes. This means, amongst other things, that "smoking rooms" located indoors in the workplace are now a thing of the past.

Any breach of an employer's rules on smoking would constitute misconduct, the seriousness of which would depend on the particular employer's rules and on the circumstances and site of the employee's smoking. Generally, an employer would be entitled to view any incidence of an employee smoking inside the workplace as gross misconduct. Nevertheless, it will be important to make sure that in-house rules and procedures make this clear.

Even where an employer's policy states that any breach of smoking rules will lead to dismissal, the manager should always consider the circumstances of the individual case. For example, in *O'Connell v Marks and Spencer plc COIT 2982/23,* the company, who operated a very strict no-smoking policy, dismissed a night-shift security guard after he was caught on a CCTV camera smoking outside the store where he worked during a break in his 12-hour night shift. The employment tribunal found that the employer had automatically implemented their policy without properly considering the facts of the particular case, and that the employee's dismissal was unfair. Mitigating circumstances included the fact that the employee was working a very long shift with little opportunity for a break, the incident was an isolated one, there was no safety hazard caused by the employee's smoking (as the incident took place outside), no customers saw him smoking, and he had no previous disciplinary record.

In contrast to the case against Marks and Spencer (above), an employment tribunal ruled that an employee's dismissal for smoking was fair in *Smith v Michelin Tyre plc [2007] ETS/100726/07.* The company's processes involved flammable substances and its strict no-smoking policy had been extended in advance of Scotland's smoking ban (introduced in March 2006) to cover all areas in and outside the factory, with the exception of some newly designated smoking areas outside the factory site. The new rules were well communicated to all staff. The employee was caught smoking at an open fire door in the staff locker room. Despite the fact that he had 12 years service and the fact that this was a one-off breach of the smoking policy, the tribunal found that dismissal for gross misconduct was a reasonable response, having taken into account all the circumstances.

Another challenging topic is the question of smoking breaks. Managers who have taken no action to control breaks may find that employees who smoke take a generous number of breaks to go outside to enjoy their daily quota of cigarettes. This can create disgruntlement amongst non-smoking employees who may object to other staff taking what they perceive as excessive breaks from work to which they are not entitled.

It is perfectly legitimate for managers to impose rules on when and how often employees take breaks. Managers should therefore monitor the situation to ensure that no employee takes time off work to which they are not entitled, whether for smoking purposes or otherwise. It may be necessary to issue a general reminder re-emphasising the organisation's rules on taking breaks from work, to remind individual employees that taking frequent breaks is unacceptable or even to warn them that such conduct will lead to formal disciplinary action if it continues.

Refusal to Abide by Dress Codes

Refusing to comply with an employer's dress code without good reason could provide the employer with grounds to take disciplinary action, up to and including dismissal.

The manager should, however, first seek to establish the employee's reason for refusing to comply with the dress code and be prepared to accept that there may be a valid reason for such a refusal. In particular, if the reason for refusal is linked to the employee's racial background or religious beliefs, the manager may be well advised to think carefully before imposing a disciplinary sanction. For example, a particular item of jewellery might have important religious significance for an employee who adhered to a particular religion and an instruction to remove it may be indirectly discriminatory on grounds of religion and hence potentially unlawful. This would be the case if the particular rule on dress or appearance put the particular employee at a disadvantage on grounds of religion (or racial background). If this was so, the manager would have to be very sure that the particular requirement could be objectively justified on business grounds, for example by showing that the rule was essential for reasons of safety or hygiene or necessary (and not just a personal opinion or preference) from the perspective of company image.

For example, in *Azmi v Kirklees Metropolitan Council [2007] IRLR 484,* the EAT ruled that the employer was justified in instructing a Muslim teacher of English to remove her full-face veil when teaching children in class. It had been established that when Ms Azmi wore the veil, this had an adverse effect on the children's ability to learn language skills from her, as they could not pick out the sorts of clues that would normally come from facial expressions. Additionally, her diction was not as clear as it would have been without the veil.

The employment tribunal ruled that the instruction to remove the veil whilst teaching amounted to indirect religious discrimination but that the employer was justified in its actions. The instruction was underpinned by a legitimate aim – namely to ensure the children received effective, unhindered language instruction and it was proportionate in light of that aim. Ms Azmi had been required to remove the veil only whilst teaching in class and there was no reasonable alternative course of action that the employer could have taken to achieve the aim of effective instruction for the children. The tribunal's decision was upheld on appeal.

This case demonstrates that where an employer has a specific, valid, properly thought out and objective reason for imposing a dress code or rule, managers are unlikely to be acting unlawfully when enforcing it through disciplinary sanctions. Managers should, however, be very careful not to make assumptions that any rules or requirements they are imposing on dress and appearance are justified. Employment tribunals will, if a case is brought before them, view the employer's decisions and actions in light of genuine and objective business requirements, and are unlikely to be swayed by an individual manager's personal views or preferences on the matter.

MISUSE OF COMPANY RESOURCES

Different organisations take very different views towards whether (and if so to what extent) their employees may use company resources for their own personal purposes. Examples may include use of company cars or vans, tools and equipment, materials, computer facilities, blackberries, workplace telephones and even stationery. Some organisations will have a "no personal use" policy towards some or all of these resources, whilst others may expect or condone a reasonable degree of personal use.

Where a manager knows or suspects that a particular employee is using company resources for personal purposes and believes that such conduct may constitute a disciplinary offence, they should investigate the facts and then set up a meeting with the employee to put the facts to them and establish their side of things, including establishing to what extent, if at all, the employee was aware of the applicable rules.

In *John Lewis plc v Coyne [2001] IRLR 139,* the employee, who had worked as a clerk for over 13 years and had a clean disciplinary record, was summarily dismissed for using her workplace telephone for personal calls contrary to the company's policy. The policy imposed a complete ban on employees using office telephones for personal calls and stated that breaches of the policy would normally lead to dismissal. The manager's investigation showed that, over a period of one year, 111 calls had been made from the employee's office telephone to three private numbers at a total cost of around £37.00.

The EAT upheld the employee's claim for unfair dismissal, pointing out that, although it would have been quite proper for the employee to be subjected to disciplinary action for breaching the company's policy on telephone use, it was not reasonable to treat the matter automatically as one of gross misconduct justifying summary dismissal. There was no evidence to suggest that the employee would have realised that her personal use of the telephone would be regarded as gross misconduct. In cases of this nature, managers should:

- Investigate and review all the circumstances of the case;

- Measure the extent of the employee's misuse of resources, for example, the number of occasions on which resources have been misappropriated;

- Investigate the employee's motive(s) for using company resources for personal purposes;

- Consider whether the employee could or would reasonably have known that their use of company resources would be viewed as misconduct;

- Consider mitigating factors, for example in the *Coyne* case (see above), some of the employee's personal calls were to her husband around the time she had suffered a miscarriage;

- Consider the employee's length of service and previous disciplinary record;

- Refrain from automatically applying disciplinary procedures irrespective of the circumstances, even where the company's policy and/or rules say clearly that a breach of the kind committed by the employee will lead to disciplinary action or dismissal.

BULLYING, HARASSMENT /ABUSIVE BEHAVIOUR

It is generally accepted nowadays that bullying and harassment in the workplace is a major problem and one which employers are entitled to take very seriously through the adoption of policies aimed at stamping out such behaviour. Any instance of alleged bullying or harassment brought to a manager's attention should be investigated and dealt with promptly, efficiently and fairly with input from HR department if the organisation has one. Similarly, the use of abusive language at work may be viewed as misconduct depending on a number of factors:

- The employer's rules (if any) on the use of potentially offensive language or swearing.

- The working environment and culture, for example the perception of what is acceptable in an office environment may be different from what is acceptable on a construction site. That is not to say that abusive language is acceptable on a construction site (or in any other workplace) but rather to indicate that different employers may have different expectations of their employees and may choose to apply different standards.

- The circumstances in which the abusive language was used. For example, a few swear words uttered in the course of discussing a difficult work issue would be viewed very differently from an instance of an employee swearing directly at their manager in an abusive manner.

- The manner and tone in which the particular language was used, for example whether it was uttered jokingly or aggressively;

- Whether and to what extent the employee who used unacceptable language was provoked;

- The effect of the abusive language. If an employee's bad language had a detrimental effect on working relationships or on morale, or genuinely upset a colleague, then it may well be regarded as misconduct justifying a warning.

In *Ogilvie v Neyrfor-Weir Ltd [2003] EAT 0054/02,* a senior employee in an oil-related company succeeded in a claim for constructive dismissal following his resignation on account of being sworn at by his manager in an aggressive, abusive and threatening manner on two occasions. The abuse occurred when the employee made a request to be excused from making a business trip overseas for family reasons.

In another case, *Horkulak v Cantor Fitzgerald International [2003] IRLR 756,* the High Court upheld a claim for wrongful constructive dismissal brought by a senior broker who had resigned part-way through his three-year fixed-term contract on account of his manager's persistent bullying behaviour and swearing. The employer attempted to put up a defence by arguing that abusive expressions and swear words were part and parcel of the particular workplace, and that such behaviour was acceptable in the context of a fast moving, high pressure environment and a high level of pay to compensate. The Court disagreed and held that the manager had not been entitled to "assert his authority by the use of foul and abusive language", irrespective of the fact that there were some serious performance issues to be addressed. The case received considerable publicity at the time on account of the high level of damages awarded to the claimant, which amounted to just under one million pounds.

Disobedience

Clearly if an employee refuses to carry out instructions, this could give rise to a disciplinary warning, or even dismissal, if the refusal is in breach of contract or could reasonably be viewed as conduct that amounts to serious insubordination. There will be two key issues for the manager to investigate:

- Whether the instruction itself was legitimate and reasonable in all the circumstances; and

- Whether the employee had a valid reason for refusing to obey the instruction.

Even if an instruction falls within the range of duties that the employee is contractually obliged to do, the employee's refusal to carry it out may nevertheless be justified, depending on the reason for their refusal. For example, in *Davies v Jack Troth t/a Richards Transport [1987]* the dismissal of an HGV driver who refused to comply with an instruction to stay away overnight when a fault developed in his vehicle was judged to be unfair. Even though the employee's contract allowed for overnight stays, the instruction to stay away was unreasonable because the employee had neither the clothes nor the money to equip him for an overnight stay.

ALCOHOL AND DRUGS OFFENCES

If a manager becomes aware that an employee's performance, conduct or attendance at work may be affected by alcohol or drugs, they should first and foremost try to establish whether the problem is one of genuine ill-health, namely an addiction to alcohol or an illegal substance, or one of misconduct.

Drugs or Alcohol Addiction

If it is established that an employee has an addiction to a particular substance or to alcohol, (whether through a medical report or through the employee admitting that they have a problem) the manager should treat the matter as one of "capability" and not misconduct. This means that the manager should:

- Recognise that the employee has a genuine illness;

- *Afford the employee all the benefits that would normally be granted to other employees under the organisation's sickness absence policy;*

- *Allow reasonable time off for medical treatment, rehabilitation, counselling, etc;*

- *Refrain from disciplining or dismissing the employee on account of their illness.*

Dismissal of an employee who is addicted to alcohol or drugs would be unlikely to be fair unless and until the employer had exhausted all other possibilities. An exception to this principle would occur if the employee was to commit an act of serious misconduct at work as a result of being under the influence of drink or drugs. In this case, taking a decision to dismiss the employee may be fair, depending always on the circumstances of the case and the manner in which the dismissal was handled.

The matter can, however, be regarded as misconduct if the employee:

- *Refuses to accept they have a problem with drugs or alcohol;*

- *Refuses or fails to respond to the opportunity for support or rehabilitation, or improves for a while, then lapses back;*

- *Is guilty of occasional heavy drinking or drug taking which adversely affects attendance, performance or conduct.*

In these circumstances, the employer's normal disciplinary procedure should be followed. It will, however, be very important to make the employee aware that any instances of unsatisfactory attendance, performance or conduct caused by alcohol or drugs will be regarded as misconduct. In other words, the employee needs to be clearly informed at what point in time the employer will begin to treat any inappropriate conduct as misconduct leading to disciplinary action, rather than as a symptom of illness.

If there is any uncertainty, the manager should normally give the employee the benefit of the doubt initially and regard the matter as an ill-health issue.

Misuse of Alcohol or Drugs at Work-Related Functions

An employee who uses illegal drugs or drinks alcohol whilst at work will clearly be committing an act of misconduct, unless (in the case of alcohol) it is a custom and practice in the particular organisation for such conduct to be condoned. Furthermore, the employee will be committing a crime if they use or distribute illegal drugs at work.

A more difficult problem will arise in the case of an employee becoming very drunk or using drugs at a work-related function held away from the workplace and attended on a voluntary basis in the employee's own time. Nevertheless, such conduct can give rise to disciplinary action up to and including dismissal provided the circumstances justify such action. The position will be clearer for the manager (and thus easier to tackle) if the employer has a policy and rules that make it clear that inappropriate behaviour at work-related functions or any conduct outside of work that may bring the employer's name into ill repute will be regarded as misconduct leading to disciplinary action up to and including summary dismissal.

Over-indulgence in alcohol at a work-related function would normally only constitute misconduct if it led to unacceptable behaviour, for example aggression, abuse or fighting. Taking drugs on the other hand is illegal, and so is more likely to be regarded as a form of workplace misconduct when occurring at a work-related event.

Taking Drugs Outside of Work

If it is discovered or suspected that an employee is using illegal drugs outside of work in their own time, the position is somewhat complex. For disciplinary action or dismissal to be fair, the employer would have to be able to show that there was a connection of some kind between the person's employment and the off-duty drug-taking. Such a connection may arise in any of the following circumstances:

- *Where the employer's rules provide for disciplinary action and/or dismissal for out-of-work drug taking.*

- If the employee's conduct makes the employee unsuitable, or unsafe, to carry on in their job. Examples could include where the employee works with machinery, has responsibility for the care of others (such as a company driver) or needs to maintain intense concentration, thus giving rise to a tangible safety risk if the employee's capacities may be impaired by the use of drugs.

- *If there is a loss of trust and confidence in the employee, particularly relevant in circumstances where a senior employee has taken illegal drugs in the presence of junior colleagues;*

- *If the association with drugs is likely to bring the organisation's name into ill-repute, which would be particularly likely where the employee's job takes them into contact with clients or members of the public.*

It is important to note that an employee who has committed a drugs offence outside of work cannot be automatically (fairly) dismissed solely on the grounds that they have been accused of an offence, remanded in custody or even convicted. Even in this situation, there must be a tangible link between the employee's drug taking and their employment if a dismissal is to be fair. Further information on conduct outside of work can be found in chapter 4.

Abuse of Alcohol

If an employee's off-duty drinking begins to affect attendance, performance or conduct, the manager would be entitled to embark on a process of investigation and subsequent disciplinary action, unless the employee is an alcoholic in which case the matter should be handled under the heading of "capability" as explained above under "Drugs or Alcohol Addiction".

What form of disciplinary action is appropriate will depend on the circumstances and the consequences (or potential consequences) of the employee's drinking. A first offence would not normally be sufficient to justify dismissal, unless the employer's rules specified otherwise.

The most appropriate course of action for a manager to take in circumstances where it is known or suspected that an employee is under the influence of alcohol at work would be to send the employee home immediately (taking care that the employee does not drive) and commence disciplinary proceedings when the employee has sobered up and returned to work.

KEY POINTS

Managers should:

- When dealing with lateness, take care to establish whether or not the employee's poor timekeeping is within their control.

- Regard incidences of mistakes or apparent carelessness as misconduct only where it is clear, following investigation, that the unsatisfactory work standards are not due to factors outside the employee's control, for example lack of training.

- Where an employee is perceived to have a bad attitude, identify specific examples of the employee's conduct that have caused the manager to form this view in order to put these points to the employee directly at an interview.

- When dealing with a breach of health and safety rules, investigate the circumstances thoroughly and take all factors into account before deciding what (if any) disciplinary action to take against the employee.

- Be alert to the possibility of employee abuse of e-mail and the internet.

- Control smoking breaks to a reasonable level so as to ensure that no employee takes excessive time off work.

- Seek to establish the reason for an employee's refusal to comply with a dress code and give fair consideration to any reasons that are linked to the employee's racial background or religious beliefs.

- Where the manager knows or suspects that an employee is using company resources for personal purposes and believes that such conduct may constitute a disciplinary offence, investigate the facts and set up a meeting with the employee to put the facts to them and establish their side of events.

- Take any complaint of bullying or harassment very seriously and investigate and deal with it promptly, efficiently and fairly with input from HR department if the organisation has one.

- Where an employee refuses to carry out instructions, review objectively whether the instruction itself was legitimate and reasonable and whether the employee had a valid reason for refusing to obey the instruction.

- Try to establish, where a manager becomes aware that an employee's performance, conduct or attendance may be affected by alcohol or drugs, whether the problem is one of genuine ill-health, namely an addiction to alcohol or drugs, or one of misconduct.

- Where an employee has an addiction to alcohol or illegal drugs, recognise that the employee has a genuine illness, afford them all the benefits that would normally be granted to other employees who are ill and refrain from disciplining or dismissing the employee on account of their illness.

CHAPTER 4
DEALING WITH SERIOUS MISCONDUCT
BOTH IN AND OUT OF WORK

INTRODUCTION

This chapter aims to explore the meaning of gross misconduct and how a manager should deal with instances of gross misconduct at work. Some other difficult issues are also discussed, specifically how to respond where misconduct is suspected but not proven, and the appropriate course of action to take if an employee commits an act of misconduct, or even a crime, outside of work.

WHAT CONSTITUTES GROSS MISCONDUCT?

Gross misconduct is a single act of misconduct which is serious enough on its own to breach the relationship of trust and confidence or otherwise breach the contract of employment and thus justify the employee's immediate dismissal. Where an act of gross misconduct has been committed, it is irrelevant whether or not the employee has received previous warnings for any similar behaviour, or whether or not the employee has a history of misconduct.

There is no legal list of what constitutes gross misconduct, and it is up to each employer to define (and communicate) what type of behaviour will be regarded by the organisation as serious enough to constitute gross misconduct. Clearly certain behaviour would always constitute gross misconduct, for example stealing from the employer, whilst other conduct may be borderline, or may be regarded as gross misconduct in one workplace, but not in another. The types of behaviour commonly listed in employers' rules may include:

- Fighting or striking another person in the course of employment;

- Theft of money or company property;

- Fraud or falsification of documents such as timesheets, expense claims, etc;

- Wilful, malicious or negligent damage to company property or equipment;

- Gross negligence in carrying out duties;

- Bullying or harassment of a colleague;

- Rudeness, swearing or offensive behaviour;

- Failure to obey reasonable instructions for no good reason;

- Unauthorised use of confidential information, including the disclosure of such information to outside sources without permission;

- Working for another employer without permission, where the nature of the work could potentially damage the business interests of the company;

- Doing paid work elsewhere whilst off sick;

- Serious breach of health and safety rules;

- Attending work under the influence of alcohol or illegal drugs;

- Smoking on company premises;

- Refusal to attend a medical examination with an occupational doctor when asked to do so;

- Driving a company vehicle without permission;

- Serious misuse of computer, e-mail or internet facilities

- Raising a grievance or making an allegation maliciously.

It is important to note that, just because a particular type of conduct is listed in an employer's rules as gross misconduct, it does not automatically follow that a dismissal for that reason will be fair. It is open to the employer to exercise its discretion in favour of the employee to impose a lesser sanction, for example a final written warning.

Similarly, just because a particular type of behaviour is *not* listed, this does not mean that the employee cannot be dismissed. It is usual for employers' disciplinary rules or procedures to include a statement to the effect that the list of conduct viewed as gross misconduct is not exhaustive. The key issue is whether the employee's conduct, viewed in light of all the relevant circumstances, can reasonably be interpreted as conduct that has fundamentally breached the employment relationship, making it unreasonable for the organisation to continue to employ the employee.

Whether or not an employee's behaviour constitutes gross misconduct will depend on a number of factors such as:

- The employer's rules (or absence of rules) covering the particular type of conduct;

- The extent to which the employee was aware of those rules;

- The terms of the employee's contract of employment;

- The employee's conduct as measured against the rules;

- The reasons for the employee's conduct and any mitigating factors;

- The context of the employee's conduct;

- The employee's position, status and length of service.

The Meaning and Legal Status of Summary Dismissal

Where an employee is found to have committed an act of gross misconduct, it will normally be fair for the employer to dismiss the employee summarily. Summary dismissal means simply dismissal implemented with immediate effect, i.e. without notice or pay in lieu of notice. Gross misconduct on the part of the employee is the only circumstance in which an employer may lawfully dismiss an employee without notice or pay in lieu. Summary dismissal thus brings employment to an end on the date it is communicated to the employee, with all pay and benefits under the contract terminating straight away.

Wages up to the last date the employee worked and any outstanding holiday pay due under the *Working Time Regulations 1998* must, however, be paid.

It is very important to note that summary dismissal does not mean instant dismissal. The employer must still follow through certain procedures prior to taking the decision to dismiss the employee (see next section). A failure to act reasonably will render the dismissal unfair, irrespective of the nature or seriousness of the employee's misconduct.

Employers should always ensure, before implementing a summary dismissal, that the specific instance of misconduct giving rise to dismissal is really serious enough, when viewed objectively, to justify the penalty of summary dismissal.

FAIR PROCEDURE WHEN DEALING WITH GROSS MISCONDUCT

As with all instances of employee misconduct, the manager dealing with the matter must take care to follow any in-house disciplinary procedure fully and fairly. Irrespective of the seriousness of the employee's misconduct, natural justice must be done. The employee has the right to be judged only after a thorough and unbiased investigation into the facts of the case has taken place and the right to challenge the evidence against them and/or explain their conduct at a properly convened disciplinary interview.

Managers who find themselves in the position of having to tackle an instance of suspected or proven gross misconduct should therefore follow through the relevant steps and guidance provided in chapter two.

Suspension from Work

Where management suspects or believes that an employee has committed an act of serious misconduct, it is usually advisable to suspend the employee from work temporarily until the matter can be fully investigated and a disciplinary interview convened. Suspension should be for as short a period as possible.

Suspension from work in these circumstances should normally be with full pay unless the particular employer has in place a contractual rule that authorises them to suspend without pay in disciplinary circumstances. Suspension without pay is always a risky course of action to take for two reasons:

- It could lead to the inference that the manager has pre-judged the employee, i.e. assumed that they are guilty of the alleged offence, thus leading to the conclusion that the ensuing process of investigation and disciplinary action is tainted with bias.

- The employee may be able to pursue a claim for unlawful deduction from wages at an employment tribunal.

Nevertheless, where the nature of an employee's alleged misconduct is such that, if proven, it would lead to the employee being dismissed, or where the employer's trust and confidence in the employee has been seriously cast into doubt, it is advisable to remove the employee from company premises to allow management the opportunity properly to investigate the alleged offence, gather the facts and prepare to hold a formal disciplinary interview with the employee.

Naturally the employee should be informed clearly as to:

- The grounds on which they are being suspended;

- How long the suspension is likely to last;

- That the suspension is not an indication of assumed guilt, nor a punishment;

- The fact that there will be a full opportunity for them to explain their version of events in due course at an interview.

Witness Statements

In the course of investigating an employee's alleged misconduct, it may be that other employees need to be interviewed to establish whether they saw or heard anything relevant to the matter under investigation.

An employee who has been witness to a colleague's misconduct may or may not be willing to provide a statement to the employer about what they observed. They may be willing to do so only if the manager promises to keep their identity a secret. This may be understandable as the employee may genuinely fear retribution if the accused employee learns that they spoke out against them.

If the employee is willing to give a written statement only on condition that their identity is withheld from the employee under investigation, the employer should respect that wish.

Conversely, there is a duty on the employer to provide the accused employee with as much information as possible about what they are accused of, including all the available evidence against them. This is in order that the employee may have a fair opportunity to challenge or refute the evidence. If an employee is dismissed without first having been given the opportunity to challenge or refute all the relevant evidence against them, their dismissal is likely to be unfair.

In *Linfood Cash and Carry Ltd v Thomson and ors EAT[1989] ICR 518,* the EAT decided that employers were under a the duty to provide an accused employee with as much information as possible, including details of the time and place of any observation or incident, and to give them copies of any witness statements, made anonymous if necessary.

In such a case, the manager has a number of choices as to how to treat the witness statements, depending on what action is necessary to conceal the witnesses' identity:

- Copy the statement in such a way as to conceal the witness' name;

- Edit the statement so as to remove any elements that would identify the witness;

- Re-write the statement in order to remove any details that might identify the witness;

- If there are a number of witness statements, write a summary of the key points of all of them together in one document.

In reviewing any statements provided by witnesses, the employer should consider a number of factors, including:

- The employment record and background of the witness;

- Whether the witness has any reason to fabricate or distort evidence, for example to protect their own interests, or because they bear a grudge against the employee;

- What weight can reasonably be given to the witness' evidence, which will in turn depend on (amongst other things) whether they were in a position to observe the employee's alleged misconduct clearly and accurately;

- Whether a witness' account of an incident concurs with that of other witnesses.

There is no statutory right for an employee against whom witness statements have been made to be allowed to question or challenge the witnesses. Nevertheless, the manager may wish to consider this course of action if it is considered appropriate and if the witnesses are willing to attend the disciplinary interview and have their evidence questioned.

Similarly, there is no general principle of law that an employee must always be shown copies of witness statements concerning the allegations against them, so long as the employee is fully and clearly informed of the content of the statements and given a full opportunity to respond. The very least the manager should do therefore, is to inform the employee of the contents of all witness statements in advance of the disciplinary interview, and allow them the opportunity to respond to the evidence at the interview itself.

A final point to note on witness statements is that employment tribunals have the authority to compel employers to disclose documents, including witness statements, if they consider them necessary for the fair disposal of the case before them. Ultimately, therefore, it is not possible for a manager to guarantee to a potential witness that their identity will never be disclosed. Reassuringly, however, in the case of *Asda Stores Ltd v Thompson and ors [2004] IRLR 598*, the EAT held that witness statements could, if there was a compelling reason justifying it, be anonymised, edited or re-written prior to the tribunal hearing in order to conceal the informants' identities.

Dealing with Complaints from Customers about an Employee

If a manager receives a complaint from a customer (or other outside person) in which it is stated or implied that a particular employee has behaved in an inappropriate manner, then clearly the manager has a responsibility to investigate and follow through on the alleged misconduct. This will be important from the point of view of the organisation's relations with its customers and their general reputation.

As explained above in the section titled "Witness statements", it is essential that an employee accused of misconduct should be given all the details of the case against them, so that they may challenge or refute any allegations of improper conduct. It follows that the manager should inform the employee of the nature and extent of the customer's complaints, and allow them the opportunity to respond. This may be done by convening an investigatory meeting initially to put the facts to the employee and establish their side of the story. The manager will subsequently be in a position to decide whether or not there are grounds to invoke disciplinary action against the employee.

Communicating this information to the employee may also be of benefit to the employee personally, who, if their customer care skills are lacking in some way, may benefit from the feedback about their behaviour so that they may learn from their mistakes.

It may be advisable in these circumstances for the manager to seek the customer's consent to raise the matter with the employee, especially where the customer has sent in a written complaint. If the customer is not prepared to consent to their identity being disclosed to the employee, the manager would have to consider whether or not a satisfactory outcome could be achieved by disclosing the substance of the complaint to the employee without disclosing the identity of the customer. This may or may not be practicable.

One pitfall to avoid is making an automatic assumption that the customer's version of events is correct or fair, and/or that the employee is to blame for what happened. There is always the possibility that the customer's allegations are untrue, exaggerated or that the dissatisfaction may have arisen as a result of a genuine misunderstanding.

The manager should:

- Refrain from pre-judging the employee's conduct;

- Seek as much information as possible from the customer, in particular what specifically the employee has done or said that the customer perceived as inappropriate or unacceptable;

- Consider the character and background of the customer (if known) and whether they might be making the accusations out of malice or for some other personal reason;

- Discuss the matter with the employee in a non-accusatory manner to establish their side of events, prior to deciding whether disciplinary action is appropriate.

DEALING WITH SUSPECTED MISCONDUCT WHERE THERE IS NO PROOF

Many managers believe, understandably, that unless there is clear proof that an employee is guilty of misconduct, then dismissal is not an option open to the employer. This is, however, not the case.

One way to explain the logic of this is to examine the function of an employment tribunal when hearing a claim for unfair dismissal. Essentially, the tribunal's function is *not* to judge whether an employee was guilty or innocent of some alleged offence, but rather to determine whether the employer acted fairly in all the circumstances, i.e. whether the decision to dismiss the employee was within the "band of reasonable responses" open to the employer. To make this judgement, the tribunal will apply the "balance of probabilities" test and not the test of "proof beyond reasonable doubt".

It follows that the fairness of a dismissal for misconduct does not depend on the manager having absolute proof of the employee's guilt. Nor will the tribunal expect the manager to have demonstrated the talents of a skilled detective, lawyer or judge in the way in which they conducted the investigation and disciplinary process.

The Three-Part Test for Fairness

The key relevant principles, which were established by the EAT in the case of *British Home Stores v Burchell [1978] IRLR 379,* are that dismissal for misconduct that is suspected but not proven may be fair, provided that the employer:

- Genuinely believes that the employee is guilty of misconduct;

- Has reasonable grounds to sustain that belief;

- Has carried out as much investigation as is reasonable in all the circumstances.

The EAT stated in the *Burchell* case (one of dismissal for alleged dishonesty) that it would not be appropriate to expect an employer to examine the evidence in a criminal context in order to assess whether the matter was one beyond all reasonable doubt.

Although this case was one involving suspected dishonesty, the principles from it have come through time to be extended to other types of conduct dismissals where the employer holds a genuine and reasonable suspicion about the employee's conduct, but has no absolute proof.

DEALING WITH MISCONDUCT THAT HAS OCCURRED OUTSIDE WORK

If an employee's conduct outside work constitutes improper behaviour, or if an employee is remanded in custody, accused or convicted of a criminal offence committed outside work, this can in certain circumstances provide the employer with grounds to invoke disciplinary action against the employee, and possibly to dismiss.

When it may be Fair to Dismiss

Disciplinary action, including dismissal, will be appropriate only if one of the following applies:

- The employer's rules state expressly that certain types of out-of-work misconduct will lead to disciplinary action up to and including summary dismissal;

- The employee's conduct makes them unsuitable or potentially unsafe to carry on in their job, for example if someone employed as a shop assistant was convicted for shop-lifting in another retail store;

- The employer has genuinely lost trust and confidence in the employee's ability to fulfil their responsibilities, for example if a senior manager responsible for young staff was remanded in custody for a drugs offence outside of work;

- The employee's out-of-work conduct is such that it could damage the organisation's business interests or reputation, for example if a sales representative who is known to the employer's customers assaults someone in a public place, or where the name of an employee who has been convicted of football hooliganism appears in the newspapers (as in the case of *Post Office v Liddiard [2001] EWCA Civ 940*);

- Colleagues refuse, with good reason, to work alongside the employee, for example if an employee working alone with a colleague genuinely fears violence on account of the employee being involved in a violent incident outside of work.

Thus, if a dismissal for conduct outside of work is to be fair, there must be a clear connection between the out-of-work conduct and the person's employment.

Serious misconduct at a work-related function such as using drugs or fighting can usually be regarded as sufficiently connected to the employment relationship to justify dismissal.

What to Do if an Employee has Committed a Criminal Offence Outside Work

It is important to bear in mind that the fact that an employee has committed a criminal offence outside of work does not automatically provide the employer with grounds for dismissal, even if the employee has already been remanded in custody or convicted.

Before contemplating dismissing an employee for criminal conduct outside of work, therefore, the manager should assess all the circumstances of the particular case, and ensure normal disciplinary procedures are followed through. It is particularly important that the manager should conduct a thorough investigation into the employee's alleged conduct, and not rely solely on police investigations. This is because police investigations are aimed at gathering evidence with a view to prosecuting the person for a criminal offence, whilst the basis for the employer's investigations should be to establish whether there are reasonable grounds for a genuine belief that the employee's conduct makes them unsuitable to continue in their employment.

Guidelines for Dealing with Misconduct Outside Work

When dealing with allegations against an employee based on conduct outside of work, managers should:

- Refrain from jumping to conclusions on the basis of gossip or comments from other staff or uncorroborated media articles;

- Give the employee a full opportunity to put forward their version of events at an interview;

- Consider carefully and objectively whether the employee's out-of-work conduct is relevant in any way to their suitability to perform their work;

- Explore alternatives to dismissal, for example if an employee engaged as a driver has lost their driving licence due to a conviction for a driving offence, consider whether they can be redeployed in alternative work until they regain their licence;

- If relying on damage to reputation as justification for dismissal, ensure there is objective evidence to back this up;

- Refrain from making assumptions about on an employee's criminal behaviour if it is irrelevant to the employee's work.

KEY POINTS

Managers should:

- Recognise that there is no legal list of what constitutes gross misconduct and it is therefore up to each employer to define what type of behaviour will be regarded by the organisation as serious enough to constitute gross misconduct.

- Refrain from automatically dismissing an employee on account of gross misconduct, but instead view the conduct in light of all the relevant circumstances and background.

- Make sure, before making a decision, that the specific instance of misconduct giving rise to a potential dismissal is really serious enough to justify the penalty of summary dismissal.

- Irrespective of the seriousness of the employee's misconduct, take care to follow any in-house disciplinary procedure fully and fairly.

- Where it appears that an employee has committed an act of serious misconduct, suspend the employee on full pay until the matter can be fully investigated and a disciplinary interview convened.

- Recognise the duty to inform an accused employee of all evidence against them provided by witnesses and ideally show the witness statements to the employee, anonymised if necessary.

- In the event of a customer complaint about an employee, refrain from assuming that the employee is guilty of misconduct but instead inform the employee of the nature and extent of the customer's complaint, and allow them the opportunity to respond fully.

- Recognise that for a dismissal for suspected misconduct to be fair, there is no requirement for the manager to have established absolute proof of the employee's guilt.

- If an employee commits an act of misconduct or a criminal offence outside of work, consider carefully before taking action whether it is relevant in any way to their suitability to perform their work.

CHAPTER 5
DEALING WITH UNSATISFACTORY JOB PERFORMANCE

INTRODUCTION

Unsatisfactory job performance is one of the most common and most frustrating challenges that managers have to deal with. Its occurrence is virtually inevitable, given the differences between individuals' personal capabilities, different attitudes to work, and the different effects factors in the workplace can have on different people. Much can be achieved, however, through proper performance management techniques.

Poor performance is often the result of factors in the workplace such as new work systems being introduced or lack of effective communication, in which case the poor performance will be not the employee's fault. The manager should in this case be prepared to work with the employee to tackle the problem that is preventing them from performing to a satisfactory standard, rather than blaming the employee. In contrast, if the cause of an employee's poor performance is laziness, lack of effort or negligence, then disciplinary action will be appropriate. It is essential, however, to distinguish between the two types of situation.

Another possible scenario is that unsatisfactory job performance is caused by an employee's genuine lack of knowledge, skill or experience, i.e. the employee is simply incapable of performing a particular type of work irrespective of how hard they may try. The manager should in this case be prepared to give as much support as is reasonable to the employee to enable them to improve rather than imposing disciplinary sanctions.

EFFECTIVE PERFORMANCE MANAGEMENT

Managing performance should be an ongoing process, and should not be restricted, for example, to a once-a-year appraisal interview.

Performance management is important at all times, but becomes particularly important when an employee is not performing their job up to the standard required by the organisation.

The starting point for the manager in these circumstances is to review what the agreed standard is, and to be sure that the employee's performance is in fact falling short of this standard. Some managers impose standards of perfectionism that are far beyond the standards that are realistically required for effective performance of the job in question, and then criticise employees for not reaching these standards.

This is, of course, unfair and is likely to de-motivate a competent employee. So long as the employee is attaining the standards required by the organisation for effective performance, this should be sufficient (although this does not, of course, preclude the manager from taking steps to develop the employee further, if the employee wishes to develop). Problems with performance can often be identified through:

- Checking employees' work;

- Ongoing observation of how the employee is performing their job;

- Discussion of errors or problems at the time they occur with a view to establishing why they occurred and preventing them from occurring in the future;

- Customer feedback;

- Formal appraisal reviews.

Ideally, managers should not wait until a problem arises before they undertake discussions with the employee about performance. It is equally important to manage performance when the employee is performing well, for example by giving positive feedback and ensuring the employee knows that their skills are valued and their efforts appreciated. Managers have a duty to their employees and to the organisation as a whole, to manage their employees effectively in order to make sure they are performing to the best of their capabilities at all times.

Probationary Periods

It is commonplace for employers to place new employees "on probation" for a defined period, typically three or six months. Such probationary periods have no status in law, but represent a useful management tool to assess objectively whether a new employee is suited to the job. It is important to note, however, that any qualifying period of service required for rights and entitlements in employment starts to run from the date employment commences, irrespective of whether or not a probationary period is in place.

Where an employer operates probationary periods for new employees, it will be important to:

● Make sure each new employee understands that they are on probation, the length of the probation period and what will happen at the end of it;

● State in writing whether the employer has discretion to extend the probationary period;

● Monitor the employee's performance regularly during the probationary period;

● Offer adequate support and training to the new employee to enable them to learn the new job and achieve the required standards of performance;

● Review the new employee's performance at or just before the end of the probationary period by means of an interview between the employee and the manager.

During the end-of-probation review interview, any problems that the new employee has experienced should be discussed with a view to identifying the cause and finding a workable solution. If there is a need for further training, this too can be discussed and agreed as part of the employee's ongoing development. If it is appropriate, the probationary period may be extended to allow the employee further time to come up to the standards required, but it is usually inadvisable to extend probation more than once.

Where a new employee has performed satisfactorily during the probationary period, the manager should not overlook the need to hold the review interview, but should instead use the opportunity to tell the employee they are performing well.

The importance of sticking to agreed arrangements with regard to probationary periods was emphasised in the case of *Przybylska v Modus Telecom Ltd [2007] EAT 0566/06*. Ms Przybylska's contract stated that the notice period applicable to her during her three-month probationary period would be the statutory minimum (one week), but that once the probationary period was completed and her appointment confirmed, a longer notice period (three months) would apply. Her manager had not, however, had the opportunity to conduct her end-of-probation review or confirm her appointment, as she was on holiday at the relevant time. The review was eventually held approximately two weeks later, at which time Ms Przybylska was dismissed with one week's pay in lieu of notice.

She brought a claim for breach of contract to tribunal, arguing that she was entitled to three months notice on termination, since her period of service had extended beyond the agreed three month probationary period. The tribunal upheld the claim, ruling that the longer period of notice (three months) came into effect automatically on the date the probationary period ended. It had been open to the manager to extend the period of probation to allow for the holiday period, but this had not been done. This meant that the claimant was entitled to three months notice on termination, and not one week.

INVESTIGATING AN EMPLOYEE'S UNSATISFACTORY JOB PERFORMANCE

There are many possible causes of unsatisfactory job performance, and many of these may be factors outside the employee's control. Managers should take care not to blame an employee automatically if their performance is falling below the required standard, or assume that the unsatisfactory standards are due to the employee's lack of effort or carelessness.

Such reactions are, of course natural – it is a common trait in human beings to assume that when things go wrong, it must be someone else's fault!

Before blaming an employee for unsatisfactory performance, the manager should always seek to explore the real root cause of the employee's perceived poor performance (see below).

Shortfalls in performance can sometimes be anticipated, for example in the following circumstances:

- When major structural or organisational change has recently occurred in the workplace, or is planned;

- When new policies or procedures are introduced;

- When the methods of doing the job are changed;

- When new objectives or targets are set;

- When new staff are recruited or existing staff promoted;

- When a new member joins an existing team;

- When workplace problems arise, for example inter-personal conflict.

Distinguishing between Lack of Capability and Lack of Effort

The main aim of exploring the root cause of an employee's unsatisfactory performance (apart from the need to ensure the employee is treated fairly) will be to establish whether the unsatisfactory performance is due to the employee's lack of capability, or to lack of effort on the employee's part. It is common, and perhaps understandable, for a manager to assume, when an employee is failing to perform to the required standard, that it is due to the employee's lack of effort, when in reality this may not be the case. The problem may instead be a lack of capability.

If an employee fails to exercise due diligence in their work, or if they are lazy or negligent, the manager should treat the matter as one of misconduct and deal with it under the organisation's disciplinary procedure (see chapter 2). Disciplinary procedures are not, however, appropriate for dealing with genuine lack of capability and the manager should instead apply good performance management techniques (see below).

One of the key distinctions between lack of capability and misconduct is that an employee's lack of capability is usually outside the employee's control, whilst employees clearly do have control over their own conduct at work (although some employees may no doubt be unwilling to acknowledge this fact!). For example, if poor performance is due lack of proper training or inadequate systems of work, this is outside the employee's control. In contrast, employees have the choice as to whether to apply themselves diligently to their duties and make a reasonable effort to perform their work accurately, or alternatively to decline to apply themselves to their duties, ignore possible mistakes and blame others when things go wrong.

Definition of Lack of Capability

Lack of capability is included in the *Employment Rights Act 1996* as a potentially fair reason for dismissal. The definition of "capability" as a reason for dismissal refers to the employee's "skill, aptitude, health or any other physical or mental quality".

In *Sutton & Gates (Luton) Ltd v Boxall [1978] IRLR 486*, the EAT stated that "capability" meant an "inherent incapacity" on the part of the employee. This essentially means that the employee, however much they may strive to perform to a satisfactory standard, will be unable to do so. Conversely, if an employee fails to come up to the required standard as a result of their own carelessness, negligence or idleness, this would not constitute lack of capability, and so could be regarded as misconduct.

Provided a manager is satisfied that the reason for an employee's unsatisfactory performance is lack of capability, and assuming all necessary training and support have been provided to the employee, a dismissal may be fair, depending on all the circumstances. Employers are not expected to put up with unsatisfactory job performance indefinitely.

Lack of capability may manifest itself in a wide variety of ways at work. Some examples might be:

● The employee makes frequent mistakes, even after full training has been given.

- The employee is unable to cope with new or different methods of working, even after adequate training.

- Performance is at an unacceptably slow pace, for example deadlines are frequently not met.

- The employee is unable to understand or follow straightforward instructions.

- The employee's communication skills (verbal or written) are inadequate in relation to the requirements of the job.

- The employee is unable to establish good working relationships with colleagues or customers.

- The employee consistently fails to meet reasonable targets for no apparent reason in circumstances where other employees in similar circumstances succeed in achieving the targets.

- The employee does not have the physical ability to perform certain manual duties that form part of their job.

- The employee demonstrates inflexibility or uncooperativeness due to lack of skill (although such behaviour could also be due to lack of effort and could in that case properly be classed as misconduct).

Possible Causes of Unsatisfactory Job Performance

There are many possible causes of unsatisfactory job performance, including:

- Physical or mental ill-health, for example the employee may be taking prescribed medication which causes them to feel tired.

- Personal problems which may, understandably, affect the person's ability to concentrate.

- Lack of training, insufficient training or the wrong type of training.

- Lack of effective two-way communication, for example where no discussions have taken place about what the priorities of the job are.

- Lack of management support for the employee to tackle day-to-day problems in their work.

- Inadequate work systems which do not allow the employee to function efficiently.

- Tools or equipment that do not function properly or regularly break down.

- Unclear or inadequate policies, procedures or written guidelines, or lack of them.

- Poor or inadequate supervision from the employee's manager, for example where no feedback or encouragement is given.

- Lack of understanding of the purpose of the job, or its goals and targets - this may arise because the manager has not properly or fully explained these issues to the employee.

- Unclear or ambiguous instructions.

- A major change to the employee's job in terms of level of responsibility or duties, in particular where sufficient training has not first been given.

- Overload of work causing the employee to feel stressed. Every employee is different and whilst some people cope admirably with high volumes of work, others may simply not be able to cope.

- Unrealistic targets or deadlines which, no matter how hard the employee tries, are unachievable.

- Difficult relationships at work, for example where a colleague is failing or refusing to cooperate with the employee.

- Bullying or harassment by a colleague, which in all likelihood would render it impossible for the employee to perform effectively.

- Change, which causes most people to feel anxious and which in turn may lead to deteriorating performance.

The main point to take out of the above list is that none of these problems would be the employee's fault. Apart from the first two points on the list, the others could even potentially be the "fault" of the manager for not ensuring that the employee is equipped to perform the job to the required standard. Yet few managers would be brave enough to admit to this and instead the unfortunate employee finds that they have to shoulder the blame for the consequences of something that they are unable to do anything about.

It is essential therefore, in the event of an employee's unsatisfactory job performance, for the manager to investigate the root cause of the problem as a first step and determine whether it might fall into one of the categories above. If so, the remedy will flow from the cause, and may involve actions such as training the employee's immediate supervisor in people-management skills, coaching the employee, re-writing procedures, re-appraising the employee's goals and targets or stamping out any instance of bullying or non-cooperation from someone else.

PROCEDURE FOR MANAGING UNSATISFACTORY PERFORMANCE

If a manager has, through investigation, ruled out any of the possible causes of unsatisfactory job performance discussed in the previous section, the manager should embark on a performance management action plan.

Action Plan – an Overview

In dealing with unsatisfactory job performance, managers should:

- Investigate the root cause of the problem (see above);
- Set up a private meeting with the employee to discuss the matter;
- Explain the problem fully to the employee at the meeting;
- Ask the employee for an explanation;
- Consider mitigating factors put forward by the employee;
- Restate what is expected (do not assume that the employee knows);

- Seek to reach clear agreement on the improvement that is required;

- Agree a timescale for improvement;

- Arrange training or coaching where appropriate;

- Be supportive;

- Warn of the consequences of a failure to improve;

- Keep records;

- Schedule a follow-up meeting, and make sure it takes place.

These matters are explored further below.

STANDARD SETTING MEETINGS

A first performance management or standard setting meeting will normally be informal and so there is no need to write to the employee beforehand or offer the right to be accompanied. The main aims will be to:

- Clarify the standard of performance that the employee should be achieving;

- Identify in what ways the employee's performance is falling short of that standard;

- Identify what needs to be done to facilitate an improvement from the employee's present standard to the required standard.

During the meeting, the manager should explain clearly and specifically to the employee in what respects they are failing to meet the standards required of the job. Vague, woolly statements such as "your work is not up to scratch" will not be helpful and may result in the employee becoming defensive. The manager needs to tell the employee precisely what they are doing wrong and why it is wrong, giving specific examples. Only then can the manager expect to hold a constructive dialogue about how the employee is to change or improve. Unless the employee is made fully aware of the precise nature of the manager's dissatisfaction, it is unrealistic to expect them to take responsibility for the problem or to achieve any improvement.

The manager should, of course make sure that the employee is given a full and fair opportunity to provide any explanations for their failure to come up to the required standards, and should be willing to listen to what the employee has to say. There may, after all, be factors of which the manager is unaware that are affecting the employee's performance.

The manager should avoid assuming that employees understand everything that is expected of them. Whilst it may be obvious to the manager what the employee should be doing, it may not necessarily be obvious to the employee.

If the problem is thought to be health-related, the manager may wish to seek the employee's consent to obtain a medical report. This topic is dealt with in chapter 6. Further information about standard setting meetings is contained in chapter 1.

Communication Skills to Encourage Cooperation

The following represents some hints and tips on how managers can encourage the employee to discuss the problem in a positive light at a standard setting meeting. The key to success will be to be open and honest with the employee, without making them feel inadequate or victimised. The manager's attitude, and the language used during any standard setting meeting, should be positive and encouraging.

The manager should:

- Open the discussion in a positive way, for example by saying that the key purpose of the meeting is to address an important issue, or build on working relationships.

- Describe the behaviour that is a problem, first in general terms, for example by saying something like: "I have noticed that sometimes there are mistakes in your work". This should be stated factually and not in a critical or judgemental tone.

- Concentrate on things the employee has done (or not done), and avoid passing judgement on the employee's personality.

- Use "you did" type statements and not "you are" statements. For example, do not say "you're stupid, your work is full of mistakes", but do say "You have made three mistakes in this report and we need to work out together how you can avoid making similar mistakes in the future".

- Give specific factual examples, such as "In the last three months, you have missed your weekly report deadline seven times". Again the tone and manner should be friendly and factual and not critical.

- Explain clearly to the employee why these matters create problems.

- Check from time to time during the meeting whether the employee has understood what is being said, for example by asking the employee how they see the matter under discussion or what they believe would be the best way to tackle a particular task.

- Explain to the employee how their job performance impacts on others, for example "when you miss your deadline, that means that we are late getting the information to the client, which in turn has a negative impact on the company's reputation". Alternatively, ask the employee how they think their actions (or inactions, as the case may be) impact on others, for example "what do you think the consequences might be for the company when your work is submitted late?"

- Reassure the employee that the underlying aim of the discussion is to seek improvement, not to criticise.

- Ask open questions (why, how, what, which, when, where, who?)

- Allow time for a response and do not be afraid of a short silence. This type of meeting is inevitably difficult for both parties and it is important to be patient so as get to the root of the matter.

- Listen carefully and patiently to what the employee has to say – and try to understand from the employee's point of view why the particular problem has arisen.

- Ask the employee at a suitable moment in the interview what they enjoy about the job. Such a question may help to break down any defensiveness and encourage the employee to open up.

- Maintain a reasonable level of eye contact with the employee.

- Use the employee's name occasionally in the conversation.

- Ask the employee to agree that the issues raised do in fact constitute a problem – if such acknowledgement can be gained, then there is a reasonable chance that the employee will also agree that some sort of change in their standard of performance is required.

- Ask the employee to suggest what specifically they need to do to ensure an improvement in performance – if suggestions come from the employee, rather than from the manager, it is more likely that the employee will be committed to putting them into action.

- Offer any further suggestions which may help and encourage the employee to improve.

- Towards the end of the meeting, summarise what has been accomplished.

- Encourage the employee to summarise what has been agreed before concluding the meeting.

- Finish the discussion on a positive note, for example by reassuring the employee that their skills/experience are valued.

The manager should ensure that the tone of the interview is one of support. It is equally important that the employee does not see themselves as a victim. They need to learn from the experience in order to reduce the probability of a re-occurrence of the problem performance.

The manager should make sure, therefore that they communicate to the employee that they are on the employee's side and not just out to give them a hard time.

Agreeing an Improvement Plan

Once the nature of the problem has been identified and discussed, the manager should seek to set reasonable targets and time limits for the employee to improve to the required standard, which should be defined in measurable terms wherever possible. This should be done in consultation with the employee, ensuring that the employee's full commitment is gained.

The employee should be asked for their ideas, and there may even be occasions when the way forward involves a compromise. The manager should bear in mind that they are not the only person with ideas of how things should be done and should be willing to consider that the employee's view of matters and ideas on how change may be achieved may be very valid. All alternative courses of action should be considered and discussed, in order to find the most effective way forward.

Ultimately, however, the manager should make sure that they have made it very clear to the employee the type and level of improvement that is required. Again, specific examples should be given. At the same time, it is important to bear in mind that a "solution" imposed unilaterally on the employee is unlikely to work in the long term. Whatever solution is required to achieve an improvement in the employee's performance must be one that the employee accepts, agrees with and believes to be workable.

Considering whether Training would be Appropriate

One of the commonest causes of unsatisfactory job performance is lack of training, or inadequate training. Where it is clear that the reason for an employee's poor job performance is lack of knowledge, skill or experience, the employer should take positive steps to assess the employee's specific training needs, and then aim to meet those needs within a reasonable timescale.

Training may involve formal classroom training, in-house coaching, computer-based learning, simple supervisory guidance, or a combination of all these and other methods. The employee's views should be sought on what is most appropriate for their needs.

The provision of training will be particularly important where new technology has been introduced or where an employee's job or work methods have changed.

If an employee is not offered appropriate training to help them to reach the required standards, for example standards of speed and accuracy, any subsequent disciplinary action or dismissal is likely to be unfair.

It is important to bear in mind that individual employees' needs vary and whilst one employee may cope well and adapt quickly to new job duties or new methods of work, another may require more extensive training and coaching before they can perform to a satisfactory standard.

Keeping Records

Following on from the meeting with the employee, the manager should make and retain an accurate record of:

- The areas in which the employee is failing to perform;

- The issues that were discussed at the standard setting meeting;

- Any matters raised by the employee;

- What has been agreed regarding improvement, i.e. what the manager has agreed to do and what the employee has undertaken to do;

- The agreed timescale for improvement.

Following Up

Once all this has been completed, the manager should make a diary note to follow up at the agreed time. This will involve the manager re-appraising the employee's performance and level of improvement on that date. The manager should meet with the employee again and provide appropriate feedback on performance. A failure to follow-though on an agreed review date and re-assess the employee's performance will represent a wasted opportunity, and be likely to de-motivate the employee and lead to a relapse back to lower standards of performance.

CRITERIA FOR A DISMISSAL FOR UNSATISFACTORY PERFORMANCE TO BE FAIR

Where an employee is, ultimately, incapable of performing the job for which they were employed, it can be fair for the employer to dismiss them, provided the employer follows proper procedures and acts reasonably in all the circumstances. Chapter 8 provides further details of fair and unfair dismissal. Dismissal for unsatisfactory performance will only be fair, however, after the employee has been given an adequate opportunity, and sufficient time, to improve to the required standard.

In order for an employer to show that a dismissal for lack of capability was fair, the employee's incapability must relate to the type of work they were employed to do. This in turn will depend on the terms of the employee's contract and the duties and responsibilities laid down in their job description, if there is one. If the employee's failure to perform to the required standards is in relation to duties that fall outside their contractual duties, the employer would be unable to establish that the employee's inability to perform those duties to a satisfactory standard was a fair reason for dismissal.

Considering Transferring the Employee to Alternative Work

In attempting to resolve the problem of an employee's lack of ability to perform their job, the manager may wish, if other courses of action have not solved the problem, to consider whether alternative work exists into which the employee could be transferred.

There is no overarching obligation on an employer to create a job for an employee who is incapable of performing their job, and the extent of the employer's duty to consider redeployment will depend on a number of factors, including for example the size and administrative resources of the organisation. One exception to this principle is where the employee has a physical or mental disability under the *Disability Discrimination Act 1995,* in which case a duty to make "reasonable adjustments" to working practices, arrangements and potentially to premises exists. In such a case, the employer will be under a positive duty to take all reasonable steps to continue to employ someone whose disability means that they can no longer perform their normal job adequately. Further information about managing employees with disabilities and avoiding discrimination is contained in chapter 6.

If an employee is dismissed for lack of capability in circumstances where a suitable alternative vacancy existed, and provided the employee was willing to transfer to this alternative job, a failure to offer it would be likely to render the employee's dismissal unfair.

Transfer to another job would, however, need to be fully discussed and agreed with the employee and not imposed against their will, otherwise this could constitute a breach of contract – see chapter 9.

Where an employee has been promoted and fails to perform to a satisfactory standard in the promoted post despite having received adequate training, the employer is under no legal obligation to offer the person their old job back (unless such a guarantee has been given to the employee at the time of the promotion, or a term to that effect exists in the contract of employment). The manager should, of course, discuss the matter with the employee and make all reasonable efforts to establish whether suitable alternative employment is available.

POOR PERFORMANCE: PITFALLS TO AVOID

There are many potential pitfalls into which managers often fall in relation to the management of performance problems. Here are some of them:

- Not bothering to establish the true cause of an employee's unsatisfactory performance.

- Assuming that the employee's unsatisfactory performance is the employee's fault.

- Allowing poor performance to continue without tackling the matter, with the result that the problem may escalate from a relatively minor issue into a major catastrophe.

- Making vague, woolly statements, for example "you're not doing very well, are you" or "it's time you pulled your socks up".

- Dropping hints instead of speaking to the employee about the specific problem.

- Throwing negative generalisations at the employee such as "you're always late presenting your reports".

- Delivering personal put-downs, for example telling the employee that they are useless.

- Criticising the employee's work in front of others – which is never acceptable no matter what the circumstances.

- Failing to review performance again after the agreed timescale for improvement.

- Rating someone's performance as "satisfactory" in an annual appraisal report when it is not. This is particular risky if there is the possibility of dismissal as the satisfactory appraisals may find their way into the bundle of documents presented to an employment tribunal at an unfair dismissal hearing.

- Giving a glowing reference to someone recently dismissed for poor performance for the same reason, i.e. the dismissed employee may be able to access the document either under the subject access provisions of the *Data Protection Act 1998* or by asking the tribunal to order its disclosure for the purpose of the tribunal hearing.

KEY POINTS

Managers should:

- Recognise the importance of managing performance regularly, including at times when the employee is performing well.

- Take care not to blame an employee automatically if their performance is falling below the required standard, nor assume that the unsatisfactory standards are due to the employee's lack of effort or carelessness.

- Always seek to explore the root cause of an employee's perceived unsatisfactory performance.

- Set up a standard-setting meeting with an employee whose performance is unsatisfactory in order to clarify the standard of performance that the employee should be achieving and identify what needs to be done to facilitate an improvement to that standard.

- Use only positive and encouraging language during any standard setting meeting.

- Ensure that the general tone of any discussion about the employee's performance is one of support.

- Set reasonable targets and time limits for improvement in consultation with the employee, ensuring that the employee's full commitment is gained.

- Bear in mind that a performance "solution" imposed unilaterally on an employee without the employee's input or agreement is unlikely to work in the long term.

- Where an employee is under-performing, assess their specific training needs, and then aim to meet those needs within a reasonable timescale.

- Always follow up after a standard-setting meeting in order to review the employee's performance again at an agreed time.

- Recognise that a dismissal for unsatisfactory performance will only be fair after the employee has been given an adequate opportunity, and sufficient time, to improve to the required standard.

CHAPTER 6
MANAGING LONG-TERM ILL-HEALTH ABSENCE

INTRODUCTION

Like every other aspect of running a business, managing long-term ill-health absence is important if the organisation is to control costs, ensure efficiency and at the same time treat employees fairly and lawfully.

This chapter aims to provide guidance to managers as to the various courses of action that might be reasonable for them to take in the event that an employee is on long-term sickness absence or is ready to return to work following a long-term absence.

LONG-TERM ILL-HEALTH – FAIR AND REASONABLE TREATMENT

No employee would choose to be ill and it is reasonable for an employee (especially if they have long service with the organisation) to expect to be treated with consideration and to be provided with a reasonable level of support if their illness or injury results in them being unable to attend work. Managing long-term sickness absence requires a pro-active approach, involving:

- Regular reviews of the employee's absence;

- Fair treatment and support to the absent employee;

- Taking all reasonable steps to facilitate the employee's return to work;

- Effective and proactive management of the employee when they return to work.

The manager, in conjunction with HR department (if the organisation has one) and with input from an occupational medical adviser, should regularly review the employee's absence and state of health/fitness to work in order to establish whether there is any improvement and whether anything can be done to facilitate the employee's recovery and return to work.

Pay and other Terms and Conditions of Employment during Sickness Absence

An employee who is absent from work due to illness or injury will remain employed by the employer. There is, however, no duty on employers to pay employees their normal wages or salary if they are absent from work due to sickness. Nevertheless, many employers choose to do so and the continuation of pay in these circumstances is usually known as "occupational sick pay" or "company sick pay". The question of whether to pay occupational sick pay, and if so for how long, is for each employer to decide for themselves.

Whatever the employer's policy on this matter is, the employer must state in each employee's written terms and conditions of employment, what their entitlement to sick pay will be in the event that they are absent from work due to sickness, together with any conditions for eligibility for payment.

If the employer wishes to make the payment of occupational sick pay discretionary, it may of course do so. In this case it is strongly advisable to devise and implement clear guidelines on how managers should exercise their discretion so that consistency and fairness are more likely. In *Clark v Nomura International plc [2000] IRLR 766*, the High Court held that management discretion in relation to pay must not be exercised irrationally or perversely. This case dealt with the payment of a discretionary bonus, but the principles would apply equally to the payment (or otherwise) of occupational sick pay.

Statutory sick pay (SSP) is a separate matter. Employers are obliged to pay employees who are unable to come to work due to personal illness or injury a fixed weekly or daily rate of SSP for up to 28 weeks during any "qualifying period", provided the employee has complied with their employer's conditions for notification of absence and provided suitable evidence of their incapacity.

An employee will not qualify for SSP if their normal earnings fall below the level at which they begin to pay national insurance contributions. Otherwise, all employees will be eligible, irrespective of their length of service with the employer or whether they work full or part-time.

When the obligation to pay SSP was first introduced, employers were able to recover amounts they paid out by offsetting them against their national insurance contributions. The recoupment provisions were subsequently abolished, however, which means that employers now have to foot the bill for SSP themselves. SSP can therefore represent a substantial cost to businesses, and this provides yet another reason why long-term sickness absence should be effectively managed. It is not open to an employer to contract out of their obligation to pay SSP.

Maintaining Contact with an Absent Employee

There are a number of reasons why it is beneficial for a manager to maintain contact with an employee who is absent from work due to illness or injury:

- The employee may welcome the opportunity to be kept up to date about what is happening in the workplace.

- The employee will be reassured that their employer cares about their welfare if contact is maintained, whereas an absence of contact may lead the employee to feel isolated, rejected and forgotten.

- The manager will be more accurately informed about the employee's state of health and progress.

- The employee is more likely to return to work sooner if they feel confident that their manager has taken a genuine interest in their welfare and has a supportive attitude towards them.

Whilst some managers may (understandably) feel uneasy about the prospect of contacting an employee who is off sick, it may be vital for an employee who is ill to maintain a link with their employment, and their colleagues, and thus avoid isolation. Regular visits or phone calls from the workplace may be the person's only link to their "normal life", and may be very welcome, so long as no pressure of any kind is put on the employee. Lack of contact, on the other hand, is likely to make the employee feel unwanted or undervalued, thus potentially adding to their problems.

If the manager still has serious doubts, they could write to the employee and ask them whether they would welcome personal visits, telephone contact and/or e-mail correspondence from someone in the workplace. It may not necessarily be the manager who is the most suitable person to make the telephone calls or home visits and it may be appropriate instead to delegate this to one or more of the employee's colleagues with whom they are friendly.

Clearly, visits to an employee's home should be undertaken only with the employee's agreement and at agreed times, as turning up unannounced may be interpreted as an intrusion into the employee's privacy. The main issue is to ensure the employee feels that their employer is interested and concerned about their welfare.

Obtaining Medical Advice

The manager may, justifiably, wish to obtain medical advice as regards the employee's condition, its effects and the likelihood of a return to work in the foreseeable future. There are two routes by which the employer may obtain medical advice, either by writing to the employee's GP (with the employee's consent) or by asking the employee to agree to be examined by an occupational doctor nominated by the employer.

Medical reports from the employee's GP

The *Access to Medical Reports Act 1988* gives employees considerable rights as regards access to medical reports prepared about them for employment purposes. The Act also limits employers' rights as regards gaining access to medical reports prepared by the employee's own doctor.

Where a manager wishes to seek a medical report from an employee's (or job applicant's) GP, the following points must be borne in mind:

- It is necessary to obtain the employee's written consent before making the application to the doctor;

- The employee has the right in law to refuse to give this consent;

- The manager must also inform the employee of their rights under the Act (see below) when asking for their consent.

It is worth noting also that any contractual term purporting to require an employee to agree to the employer obtaining a report from their GP would be unenforceable, because such a term would contradict the rights given to individuals under the law.

Employees have the following rights under the *Access to Medical Reports Act:*

- To be informed by their employer *in writing* if the employer wishes to contact their GP for a medical report;

- To refuse to give consent to the employer making an application to the GP for a medical report;

- If consent is given, to gain access to the report directly through their doctor on request (once it has been prepared);

- To ask their doctor to amend the report, if they believe it is inaccurate or misleading;

- To refuse to allow the report to be passed on to the employer after it has been prepared.

It can be seen therefore that the *Access to Medical Reports Act* imposes limitations on employers in relation to their ability to obtain information from an employee's GP.

The steps the manager would have to take to seek a report from the employee's GP are therefore to:

- Write to the employee asking for their consent for the manager to write to their GP requesting a medical report;

- Include written information for the employee about their rights under the Act;

- If the employee's consent is granted, write to the doctor to request a medical report, setting out any specific information that is sought;

- If the employee has indicated a wish to gain access to the report before it is released to the employer, advise the doctor of this fact in writing along with the request for a medical report.

- Enclose with the letter a copy of the employee's consent letter, otherwise it is unlikely that the doctor will answer the manager's letter.

- Inform the employee that the request has been made.

The manager should take care to inform the doctor why medical advice is required and to provide sufficient meaningful information, for example about the employee's job duties and working environment.

Furthermore, specific questions should be asked of the doctor, for example:

- The likely length of time that the doctor thinks the employee will have to remain absent from work;

- Whether, when the employee returns to work, there is likely to be any remaining partial incapacity, for example tiredness;

- Whether the employee may be well enough to perform part-time work, or lighter duties, even if they are unable to resume their normal job on a full-time basis;

- Any recommendations that the doctor would consider helpful to the employee, for example exemption from heavy physical work.

The manager should, of course, not expect to receive details about the employee's medical condition as this is personal to the employee, but may reasonably expect to receive information and/or advice on the employee's fitness to work and any relevant effects of the employee's condition on their abilities.

Medical reports from an occupational doctor

The *Access to Medical Reports Act* does not normally apply to reports prepared by occupational doctors or in-house doctors engaged by the employer. This is because the wording of the Act refers to doctors who are or have been "responsible for the clinical care of the individual". Thus it is often easier (at least in theory) to ask the employee to agree to be examined by an occupational doctor and to obtain a medical report from that doctor on the employee's fitness to work. Additionally, in most cases an occupational doctor will have a better understanding than a GP of the employer's working environment and of any special demands or hazards (whether physical or mental) inherent in the workplace or in the employee's job.

In practice, however, the employee's consent is still required, simply because no doctor will examine a patient without the person's consent. It is helpful to the employer to include clauses in all employees' contracts to the effect that they are required, on reasonable request, to agree to be examined by an occupational doctor nominated (and paid for) by the employer and to agree to the doctor providing a confidential report to the employer. Such a clause is contractually valid, provided the wording clearly applies only to occupational doctors and not employees' own doctors.

If an employee refuses without good reason to cooperate with the employer's request to obtain a medical report, the employer is entitled to proceed to make a decision about the individual's ongoing employment based on the facts known to them at the time. In the event of a claim for unfair dismissal at tribunal, the tribunal will take into account the employee's refusal to cooperate with the employer in their investigations.

In *Elmbridge Housing Trust v O'Donoghue Court of Appeal [2004] EWCA Civ 939,* an employee whose presence at work was vital for the employer was dismissed on grounds of incapability after an absence of only three and a half months. The employee, whilst absent, had insisted that her employer should only communicate with her through her trade union representative and had repeatedly refused to cooperate with the employer in relation to requests for her consent to an occupational health adviser's examination and report.

The Court of Appeal held that the dismissal was fair. The employer was entitled to seek to clarify the reason for the employee's absence, and to try to find a solution. The employer had done all they reasonably could do to elicit medical information and, given the employee's consistent refusal to provide consent, the employer had waited for a reasonable period before dismissal.

Facilitating a Return to Work after a Period of Absence

The key aims of a manager when an employee is off sick long-term will be to:

- Support the employee in whatever ways are reasonable and practicable during their absence;

- Facilitate a return to work as soon as possible.

It is as important to manage an employee's return to work carefully and with consideration, as it is to manage their absence.

Some of the options the manager may wish to consider, in consultation with the employee might be to:

- Consider whether the employee who is unable to perform their normal job might be willing and able to do a different job, for example one that is physically less demanding or one with less pressure (see below).

- Consider a phased return to work, for example two days a week to start with, or mornings/afternoons only.

- Perhaps arrange a social visit for the employee prior to the proposed return date so that they can meet informally with colleagues and the manager.

- Discuss all the options with the employee directly.

Once it is agreed that the employee is ready to return, further actions for the manager include to:

- Discuss the employee's capabilities with them and review whether any special arrangements, support or adjustment to job duties need to be provided initially.

- Brief the employee thoroughly on their return to provide an update on company developments and departmental activities.

- Make sure the employee is given meaningful work to do as soon as possible after their return.

- Ensure the employee is not overloaded with work or faced with a mountainous backlog of work on their return.

- Recognise that the employee is likely to feel tired initially and be willing to exercise reasonable tolerance, without expecting one hundred per cent performance on the employee's first day back.

- Agree with the employee how progress will be monitored during the first few weeks or months after their return.

- Consider nominating someone to be the employee's mentor or "buddy" for the first few weeks in order to monitor the employee's well-being and provide general support.

- Take positive steps to ensure the employee feels their return to work is welcomed.

- Monitor the situation over the first few weeks to ensure the employee is coping.

Bear in mind that an employee who has been absent from work for a time (especially if their illness has been stress-related) may feel very anxious about the prospect of returning to work, and worry about how they will be treated and whether they will cope.

It will therefore be very important for the manager to take positive steps to welcome the employee back, provide support and do whatever is possible to assist their re-integration into the workplace.

Considering altering Job Duties or offering Part-Time Work

As stated above, it may be helpful to consider whether an employee who has had a lengthy period of sickness absence may benefit from being offered a return to different job duties, or even part-time working, at least initially.

Whilst these options may be beneficial to the employee, the manager should take care not to impose a solution without the employee's clear agreement. Additionally, the manager should seek medical advice on whether a particular course of action would be appropriate for the employee.

Essentially, any major change to an employee's job duties, and any change or reduction to working hours, will represent a variation to the employee's contractual terms. This means that, in order to avoid being in breach of contract, the manager must obtain the employee's express consent to the change. Provided agreement is obtained, the employer would be able to adjust the employee's wage/salary to reflect any reduction in working hours.

If agreement is not obtained, a fundamental change to any of the terms of the employee's contract would give the employee the right to resign immediately and bring a claim for constructive dismissal to an employment tribunal (subject to their having a minimum of one year's continuous service). Naturally the manager's duty is to support the employee and not to impose unwelcome changes to their contract on account of their having been ill. All proposed changes should therefore be discussed and agreed with the employee. Further details about implementing changes to employees' terms and conditions appear in chapter 9.

THE IMPLICATIONS IF AN EMPLOYEE'S CONDITION AMOUNTS TO A DISABILITY IN LAW

An employee who has a long-term medical condition may be covered by the *Disability Discrimination Act 1995*. If this is the case, the employee's manager will be responsible for ensuring that:

● They do not subject the employee to any unfavourable treatment for a reason related to their disability, unless the specific treatment can be justified in all the circumstances;

● They fulfil the duty to make reasonable adjustments to support the employee (see below).

114

The *Disability Discrimination Act* applies to all employers, irrespective of their size. The only exemption is the armed forces.

A disabled employee who suffers discriminatory treatment in the course of employment may bring a complaint of disability discrimination to an employment tribunal irrespective of their length of service. Furthermore, where a claimant is successful, the tribunal will usually order the employer to pay compensation for lost earnings and injury to feelings, and such compensation is unlimited.

Definition of "Disabled"

The definition in the Act of a disabled person is someone who "has a physical or mental impairment which has a substantial and long-term adverse effect on ability to carry out normal day-to-day activities". "Long-term" in this context means 12 months or more. "Substantial" has been described as meaning "not minor or trivial". "Normal day-to-day activities" means the things most people do fairly regularly in their every-day lives, and not the specific activities that an employee is required to undertake as part of their job.

Another important point is that a person whose impairment is fully controlled by medication will be covered by the Act, provided that the effects on their day-to-day activities would be substantial if they were not taking their medication.

It is likely that in many cases the manager will not be in a position to know whether or not the employee's condition amounts to a disability in law, since the assessment of whether a particular person is disabled from a legal perspective is a complex one. The best approach is therefore to assume that the employee may be protected by the Act and proceed accordingly. It can be dangerous to assume that an employee is not disabled just because they "look OK" to the manager, and equally dangerous for the manager not to apply their mind to the possibility that an employee who has had a lengthy period of absence (or frequent periods of short-term absence) due to an underlying medical condition is not disabled.

The Scope of the Act

The Disability Discrimination Act covers:

115

- A wide range of physical illnesses and conditions, provided they last, or are expected to last, 12 months or more;

- A wide range of mental illnesses, including many stress-related conditions;

- Other mental conditions, such as dyslexia;

- Learning difficulties;

- Progressive conditions such as Alzheimer's disease and Parkinson's, which are covered as soon as the condition is diagnosed.

- Cancer and multiple sclerosis which are automatically considered to be disabilities.

- AIDS and HIV;

- Recurring or fluctuating conditions, even during periods of remission, provided the condition is long-term and likely to recur.

- Past disabilities, where the employee is now fully recovered.

Certain conditions are expressly excluded from the Act, including addiction to alcohol, illegal drugs or nicotine.

The cause of the disability is irrelevant to the question of whether the person can claim protection under the Act.

The Duty not to Discriminate

The Disability Discrimination Act imposes a duty on employers not to treat an employee unfavourably:

- Directly on the grounds that the person is disabled or has a particular disability; or

- On grounds *related to* the person's disability, unless this can be justified.

Grounds related to disability could include any effects of the employee's disability, for example poor performance (i.e. if the disabled employee is still attending work), or of course a period of sickness absence.

The following is an example of the distinction between the two types of disability discrimination:

- Following an accident in which an employee has lost the use of their legs, the employer proceeds to dismiss that employee, just because they are now substantially impaired as regards their mobility. That would constitute direct disability discrimination, which is not open to justification and will thus be unlawful.

- In contrast, the employer first reviews the matter (including holding discussions with the employee and obtaining medical advice) and concludes that, irrespective of any reasonable adjustments, the employee would still be unable to perform their job to a satisfactory standard. A dismissal in these circumstances would be on grounds *related to* the employee's disability, namely their inability to perform the job. Assuming that there was no other job into which the employee could reasonably be transferred, the dismissal, although discriminatory, may be justified and thus lawful.

Thus, the important distinction between the two forms of discrimination is that direct disability discrimination can never be justified in law, whilst disability-related discrimination *may* be justified, provided that there is a material and substantial reason for the employer's treatment of the employee.

The Duty to Make Reasonable Adjustments

Under the *Disability Discrimination Act*, employers are under a duty to make reasonable adjustments to any "provision, criterion or practice" that the employer applies, and to physical features of premises, in order to accommodate the needs of a disabled worker (or job applicant). The phrase "provision, criterion or practice" is very wide in scope and would cover all policies, procedures, systems of work, rules and practices, whether contractual or not.

It is important for managers to bear in mind that the duty to make reasonable adjustments is mandatory, not optional. It is equally important to note that the duty to make reasonable adjustments is on the employer, i.e. it is not up to the employee to request an adjustment. Indeed there is no duty on the employee under the Act

117

voluntarily to disclose the fact that they have a disability, nor to draw the need for adjustments to the employer's attention. Naturally, if an employee nevertheless does so, the manager should be prepared to consider their submissions favourably.

The manager should aim to be proactive and:

- Speak to any employee whom they know to be disabled, or who is or has been absent from work due to illness or injury, to establish whether the employee considers that any particular adjustment would be helpful to them.

- Reassure the employee that the reason for the question is so that the employer can take steps to support the employee and at the same time meet its duty under the *Disability Discrimination Act*.

- Seek to assess, with input from a medical specialist as appropriate, the effects of the employee's condition on their ability to perform their job duties, the effects of the physical features of the workplace on the employee's capabilities, the prognosis, and the steps that the employer might reasonably take that would reduce or remove the disadvantages the employee is experiencing.

Although the duty may seem onerous, managers should note also the word "reasonable" contained in the wording of the law. Managers are obliged to make a particular adjustment only if it is reasonable in all the circumstances for them to do so.

What is reasonable will depend on many factors, including:

- The size and resources of the employer as measured against the type of adjustment proposed;

- The degree of disruption the adjustment would cause;

- The likely effect of a particular adjustment on the employee's colleagues or on customers;

- The need to abide by safety regulations and any other legislation.

Examples of Adjustments where an Employee has had a period of Sickness Absence

Some examples of adjustments to working practices that might be helpful to an employee who has a disability that has caused a period of sickness absence might include any of the following:

Adjustments to the job

- Transfer the employee to another job, for example if they are no longer able to perform their own job. This would, of course, have to be with the employee's express agreement as explained above. Alter the employee's job duties, for example by exempting the employee from performing heavy physical work, or allocating some duties to other employees.

Adjustments to working patterns or hours

- Permit part-time working for a time.

- Permit a later or flexible start time if the employee's condition (or the medication they take for it) causes disturbance to their sleep pattern or difficulty waking up in the morning.

- Vary the person's hours (temporarily or permanently) to fit in with regular medical appointments.

- Allow a disabled employee to take more time off work than would normally be acceptable.

- Adjust sickness absence procedures so that disability-related absences are discounted (although it was held in *Royal Liverpool Children's NHS Trust v Dunsby [2006] IRLR 351* that there is no absolute rule that disability-related absences must be discounted when calculating an employee's total periods of absence for the purpose of operating sickness absence procedures).

Adjustments to the place of work

- Allow the employee to work partly from home, for example to help ease them back into full-time employment. In *London Borough of Hillingdon v Morgan [1999] EAT 1493/98,* the EAT ruled that an employer had failed to comply with their duty to make reasonable adjustments because they had refused, for no good reason, to allow an employee who had been absent from work with ME to work from home temporarily to assist her transition back into full-time employment.

Adjustments to the level of support provided

- Provide additional supervision, coaching or mentoring.

- Provide additional or longer rest breaks where the employee's condition means they tire easily.

Managers should always ask a disabled employee what adjustments they believe might be helpful, and of course consult them over any adjustment that they are proposing. The disabled person will, in any event, have a better understanding than the manager of what measures would help to facilitate normal working and help them to overcome any disadvantage that their disability might otherwise cause them.

Finally, it is worth noting that the Act provides that it is not discriminatory against other employees to give special treatment to a disabled employee on account of their condition.

WHEN DISMISSAL BECOMES A REAL POSSIBILITY

It is potentially fair in law to dismiss an employee on account of genuine long-term ill-health absence. The reason for dismissal will be "lack of capability". The statutory definition of "capability" refers to the employee's "skill, aptitude, health or any other physical or mental quality".

There is no guidance in law as to the time period after which it may be fair to dismiss an employee who is absent from work due to ill-health. The key question that determines fairness (or unfairness) in a dismissal for ill-health absence, is whether in all the circumstances the employer can reasonably be expected, in light of their business requirements, to wait any longer for the employee to recover and return to work.

However, before reaching the stage where termination of an employee's employment on grounds of ill-health is contemplated, the manager should of course have looked at ways of facilitating the employee's return to work. Dismissal should be considered only as a last resort.

The Importance of Advising the Employee when Termination has Become a Possibility

It will be essential for the manager to arrange to speak to the employee at the point at which termination of employment is first considered as an option. This is because it would be intrinsically unreasonable for any employer to terminate an employee's employment without first warning them that such action was being contemplated. It is usually a sound idea for the manager to set a time limit for review of the employee's absence and inform the employee of this. For example, the manager might communicate to the employee that a review will be held in three months time and at that point a decision will have to be made regarding the employee's continuing employment with the organisation.

Examining the Effect of the Employee's Absences on the Business

Whether and when it will be potentially fair to dismiss an employee on the grounds of long-term absence will depend on a number of factors, in particular the impact of the employee's absences on the organisation. Relevant matters would include the extent to which the absence is causing the employer operational difficulties, creating problems with customer service or adversely affecting other employees who may be required to carry the employee's workload.

For example, if the employee is employed in a senior position or in a highly specialised job in a small organisation, absence of a few months might cause serious difficulties for the employer. In contrast if a clerical worker in a large organisation falls ill and is absent for a period of two years (for example), this may cause no disruption or difficulty for the business at all as they may easily be able to arrange for the work to be covered, for example by recruiting a temporary worker from an employment agency.

Background Factors that will Impact on Fairness

In the event that an employee dismissed on the grounds of long-term sickness absence brings a claim for unfair dismissal to an employment tribunal, the tribunal will consider firstly whether the reason for dismissal, namely the employee's lack of capability, was sufficient to justify the termination of their employment by the employer. Factors that will be relevant to the determination of this question include:

- The size and resources of the organisation;

- The effect of the employee's absences on the organisation's business and on colleagues (see above);

- The urgency and importance of the employee's work;

- The feasibility of employing a temporary replacement to cover the work;

- The length of the absence so far;

- The likelihood of an improvement in the employee's health in the foreseeable future;

- Where appropriate, how the employer has treated other employees on long-term sickness absence in the past;

- The availability of suitable alternative work as an alternative to dismissal.

Procedure for Fair Dismissal on the Grounds of Long-Term Sickness Absence

Incapability due to genuine ill health should never be dealt with by using disciplinary procedures. Such an approach might upset the employee and even, in certain circumstances, lead to an exacerbation of their illness. Nevertheless certain aspects of the disciplinary procedure, for example informing the employee of the outcome of a failure to improve, may be adapted to form part of a "capability procedure". A well-designed and properly implemented capability procedure may result in the employee's dismissal, but will achieve the necessary outcome without the unpleasantness of a disciplinary approach.

For a dismissal to have a chance of being fair, the manager should ensure that all the following steps have been carried out. The manager should:

- Conduct a review of the employee's absence and its effects on the business.

- Seek to obtain up-to-date medical advice about the employee's fitness to work and in particular whether there is any likelihood of a return to work in the foreseeable future.

- Write to the employee, advising them that a review is being carried out and inviting them to attend a meeting. The letter should make it clear that the circumstances of the employee's ongoing absence are such that termination of employment is now a possibility.

- Ensure the timing and location of any meeting is reasonable and suitable for the employee.

- Grant the employee the right (if they wish) to be accompanied at the meeting by a colleague or trade union official of their choice.

- Assuming it is possible to hold a meeting, discuss the options with the employee, for example if a transfer to different job duties might be a possibility as an alternative to dismissal.

- Be prepared to take on board any representations put forward by the employee as regards their absence and likely return to work.

- After the meeting (and not before), take the decision on whether to terminate in light of all the circumstances.

- Communicate the decision to the employee in writing.

- Allow a right of appeal against a decision to dismiss the employee.

Ultimately, dismissal may be fair for ill-health sickness-absence, but it will only be so if the circumstances justify it and if the employer has acted reasonably towards the employee throughout.

In *East Lindsey District Council v Daubney [1977] IRLR 181*, the EAT made it clear that for a dismissal on the grounds of an employee's ill-health to be fair, the employer must first consult with the employee in order to discuss the circumstances and establish the true medical position.

It will also be necessary to ensure the employee is given their full period of notice as required in statute and under their contract of employment – see chapter 8.

Interestingly, the Court of Appeal ruled in *Burlo v Langley and anor [2007] IRLR 145*, that where an employee's contract specifies that only statutory sick pay will be payable during periods of sickness absence, there is no entitlement to full pay during the notice period if the employee is unable to work it due to sickness or injury (although the Court acknowledged that to pay full pay during notice would represent good industrial practice).

There is, however, a little-known provision in the *Employment Rights Act 1996* which states that where the employee's contractual period of notice is the same as, or no more than a week longer than, the required period of statutory notice, then the employee is entitled to be paid full pay if they are absent from work due to sickness or injury during the notice period.

KEY POINTS

The manager should:

- Recognise that there is no duty on employers to pay employees their normal wages or salary if they are absent from work due to sickness, although statutory sick pay must almost always be paid.

- Ensure reasonable contact is maintained with an employee who is absent from work due to illness or injury.

- Seek to obtain medical advice as regards the employee's condition, its effects and the likelihood of a return to work in the foreseeable future.

- Adhere to the provisions of the *Access to Medical Reports Act 1988* when seeking to obtain a medical report from an employee's GP.

- Aim to support an employee who is absent from work due to long-term illness in whatever ways are reasonable and practicable, and to facilitate a return to work as soon as possible.

- Once the employee has begun to recover, consider a phased return to work if that would be helpful to the employee.

- When the employee returns to work, discuss their capabilities with them and review whether any special arrangements, support or adjustment to job duties need to be provided initially.

- Ensure an employee who has been absent for a lengthy period is not overloaded with work when they return.

- Consider, where an employee is unable to perform their normal job, whether transfer to alternative duties might be an option and discuss all possibilities with the employee.

- Recognise that an employee who has a long-term medical condition may be protected by the *Disability Discrimination Act 1995.*

- If an employee's condition amounts to a disability in law, ensure that they are not subjected to any unfavourable treatment for a reason related to their disability, unless the specific treatment can be justified in all the circumstances.

- Where an employee is disabled, be proactive in considering what adjustments to the employee's working arrangements or practices might be reasonable and ask the employee what adjustments they think might be helpful to them.

- Consider dismissing an employee on grounds of long-term ill-health absence only as a last resort and only after ways of facilitating the employee's return to work have been fully examined and found to be impracticable.

- Get up-to-date medical advice, in particular about the likelihood of the employee returning to work in the foreseeable future, before considering dismissal.

- Arrange to speak to the employee as soon as termination of employment starts to be considered as an option.

- Make sure that proper procedures are carried out prior to the termination of an employee's employment on the grounds of long-term ill-health absence.

CHAPTER 7
DEALING WITH FREQUENT, PERSISTENT ABSENCES

INTRODUCTION

Where an employee has a poor attendance record based on frequent and/or persistent short-term absences, this can cause considerable disruption to the smooth running of any organisation and will often create severe difficulties for the employee's manager and fellow-workers. Furthermore, the cost of casual absenteeism can be substantial.

In essence, the effective management of short-term absence requires managers to strive to achieve a reasonable balance between (on the one hand) the needs of the business and (on the other hand) the "right" for the employee to be afforded an appropriate degree of support if illness or other factors genuinely beyond their control have led to a high level of short-term absenteeism.

This chapter aims to provide guidance to managers on how to manage, control and reduce short-term absenteeism.

MONITORING SHORT-TERM ABSENTEEISM

It is sound practice for employers to devise and implement a policy and procedure covering the steps that will be taken to monitor employees' periods of absence from work. The steps of the procedure will fall broadly into two stages:

1. Speaking with the employee each time they return to work after an absence, however short

2. Carrying out a review whenever an employee's absences reach a defined trigger point.

The policy and procedure should of course be properly communicated to all staff and applied reliably and consistently on all occasions.

Managing Individual Absences

An absence management procedure should be instigated as soon as an employee phones in sick. The procedure should specify whom the employee must telephone if they are unable to come to work, and within what time-scale. It should also state that the employee must telephone personally, unless this is impossible or impracticable. The telephone call should normally be to the employee's immediate supervisor or line manager and employees should not, for example, be permitted to leave vague messages with the employer's receptionist or on a colleague's voicemail.

Whoever takes the call should create a record (perhaps using a pre-printed form) of:

- Whether it was the employee personally who phoned, or someone else who made the call on their behalf;

- The reason given for the employee's inability to attend work;

- How long the employee expects to be absent;

- The date and time of the call.

This form should be placed on a file and will form the start of an absence management record. This form could also be used for the purpose of initiating payment of statutory sick pay.

It is helpful also if the procedure covers what will happen if, when the employee phones in, the person to whom they need to speak is unavailable. In these circumstances, that person should, when they receive the message that the employee called, telephone the employee back in order to obtain or verify the necessary information (as above). Such a call is not intrusive as it represents a simple courtesy to return a call that could not be taken at the time.

Conducting Return-to-Work Interviews

To deal effectively with instances of frequent short-term absences, the manager should adopt a stringent return-to-work interview procedure, together with a system of self-certification, so that each time the employee is absent from work, the absence is discussed directly with them, and recorded. A return-to-work interview should be conducted every time the employee is unexpectedly absent, irrespective of the length of the absence. This has four key advantages for the employer:

- Knowing that they will have to face their manager and explain their absence may act as a disincentive for the employee to take casual days off in the future.

- It will enable the manager properly to monitor the employee's absenteeism and the reason(s) for it, and to recognise if and when a point has been reached where the level of absence has become unacceptable.

- It will allow the manager to investigate and establish whether there are any factors in the workplace that may be causing or contributing to the employee's absences.

- The manager will be in a strong position to determine whether the employee needs any specific support.

The return-to-work interview should be informal, but more than just a "corridor chat". The manager should invite the employee to their office and ensure the discussion is private and confidential. They should also make sure that the employee understands that the interview is *not* part of the disciplinary process, but is rather for the purpose of monitoring absenteeism and checking whether the organisation can do anything to support the employee, should there be an underlying problem. Because this type of interview is informal, the right to be accompanied will not, technically, apply.

At the interview, the manager should ask the employee some key questions, such as:

- The reason for the absence - without of course requiring the employee to disclose personal medical details;

- Whether the employee visited their GP;

- How the employee is feeling now;

- If appropriate, whether anything at work caused or contributed to the absence;

- Whether there is anything the manager can do to support the employee.

If there should be any discrepancy between the reason for absence stated at the return-to-work interview and what was said earlier when the employee (or their partner, mother, etc) first notified the manager that they were unable to come to work, then the manager will be able to spot the discrepancy and ask the employee to explain it.

The manager should make a record of the employee's answers to the questions asked and a short and simple pre-printed form may be devised for this purpose. The notes on the form will represent the manager's perspective on the employee's absence.

The manager should also ask the employee to complete a self-certification form at the interview and in the presence of the manager, which should then be signed by both the employee and the manager. This will represent the employee's perspective on their absence. Self-certification forms are normally used for short absences of up to one working week.

Both forms should be held on file, and the manager will need to bear in mind that the employee will have the right of access to these and any other personal documentation relating to them under the *Data Protection Act 1998*.

WHAT TO DO ONCE ABSENCES START TO BECOME FREQUENT

If an employee's absences start to be become frequent, the manager should conduct a review meeting with the employee. This review meeting will have the dual purpose of investigating whether there is any underlying cause of the frequent absences and making the employee aware that their absences have reached a level where they are beginning to represent a problem.

It is helpful to state in a company policy what levels of absence will trigger such a review in terms of:

- The total number of days absence over a period of six or 12 months;

- The number of separate occasions that the employee has been absent during the same period.

A typical example could be a trigger point reached after the employee has been absent for a total of twelve working days or has had three or more separate absences in any twelve-month period.

Potential Causes of Persistent Absence

There are many potential underlying causes for frequent, persistent absences. Some of these are:

- The employee may have an underlying medical condition or disability that flares up from time to time;

- The employee may have an unusually high vulnerability to colds, flu and/or a variety of other minor ailments;

- The employee may tend to feel excessively tired in the mornings, for example because they stay out late at night, or have another job;

- There may be recurring personal or family problems;

- The employee may be thoroughly de-motivated at work, in which case the cause of the de-motivation should be explored;

- The employee may be experiencing a level of pressure or stress at work that they feel they cannot cope with, which in turn may be due to a heavy workload, over-tight deadlines, long working hours, etc;

- There may be a specific problem at work, for example conflict with a colleague or even bullying, which causes the employee to feel that they cannot face coming into work.

It will be very important for the manager to try to ascertain the true underlying reason for repeated absences so that if there is a workplace issue that needs to be addressed, this can be brought to the fore and tackled. The manager should therefore take the time to explore with the employee whether anything in the workplace is contributing to their absences. The question should be asked sympathetically and the manager needs to take care to reassure the employee that if they are experiencing problems at work, the manager would wish to provide as much support as possible with a view to resolving the particular problem.

Planning and Setting Up a Review Meeting

Before the review meeting takes place with the employee, the manager should review the employee's absence record (i.e. the forms completed when the employee phoned in and those created at the return-to-work interview stage). In so doing, the manager should look to see if there is any pattern to the employee's absences. There may, for example, be a predominance of Monday absences or a pattern that suggests the employee goes off sick each time an important deadline is approaching. If such a pattern is identified, this should be put to the employee at the review meeting.

Other matters for investigation may include examining:

- Whether absenteeism in any particular section of the manager's department is higher than average when viewed against the level of absence within the organisation as a whole;

- Whether the rates of absence of employees performing any particular job are disproportionately high when compared to employees in other types of work;

- Whether there is any particular type of sickness absence that occurs repeatedly, and the possible reasons for this.

Having conducted any necessary background investigations, the manager should write to the employee inviting them to come to a meeting to review their absence record, explaining that their level of absence is causing concern and enclosing a note detailing the dates of all absences over the last six or twelve-month period (as appropriate). Since a meeting set up to review an employee's absences will be more formal in nature than the return-to-work interviews discussed above, the manager should offer the employee the opportunity to be accompanied at the meeting by a colleague of their choice or a trade union official, if the employee wishes.

Conducting a Review Meeting

At the review meeting itself, the manager should adopt a supportive approach towards the employee, especially if it is known that the employee has, for example, an underlying medical condition or family problems that have been affecting attendance. At the same time, the manager needs to explain clearly to the employee that continuous absences are unacceptable from the employer's perspective because of the problems they cause. The approach should therefore be one of "balance", i.e. the manager should show understanding of the employee's circumstances and needs whilst at the same time seeking to fulfil the needs of the business to ensure the work is done efficiently and on time.

At the review meeting, the manager should:

- Inform the employee that their absences have reached a level that is considered unsatisfactory and the reasons why this is the case.

- Talk to the employee about the reasons for their frequent absences – and give full consideration to any explanations and/or mitigating factors put forward by the employee.

- Ask whether anything or anyone in the workplace is causing or contributing to the employee's absences. The manager should seek to explore whether factors at work might be causing the employee stress or anxiety to the extent they find coming to work difficult. This topic is dealt with further below.

- Without asking intrusive questions, seek to establish whether some of the employee's absences are on account of personal or family problems. If this is the case, a reasonable degree of support, tolerance and sympathy would be appropriate. After all, no employee chooses to have such problems and they may be outside the employee's control, for example if a child repeatedly falls sick.

- If considered appropriate, discuss with the employee the possibility of obtaining a medical report from an occupational doctor or the employee's GP (see chapter 6). This may (or may not) reveal an underlying medical cause for the employee's absences. If the employee is unwilling to consent to the disclosure of a medical report, the manager will have to decide how to proceed based on whatever information is available.

- If any particular pattern of absence has been identified (for example a predominance of Monday absences), put the facts to the employee and ask them for an explanation, without of course making assumptions or implying that the employee's absences are not for genuine reasons. Even if the employee is unable to put forward any explanation, such a question will have the advantage of alerting them to the fact that the line manager has noticed the pattern, which may in turn deter further casual absences.

- Set reasonable targets and time limits for improvement in the employee's level of attendance and seek to gain the employee's commitment to try to achieve such improvement. The manager should of course follow up on this at the agreed time and review the employee's level of absence again. If, at this time, the employee's level of attendance has not improved to a satisfactory level, it may be appropriate to consider moving to a process of formal warnings (see next section).

- *Tell the employee in clear language what the consequences will be of a failure to improve, i.e. the employee may face formal action with a series of formal warnings and eventual dismissal. This should be stated factually, taking care that the manager does not make the statement sound like a threat.*

The aim should always be to strike a balance between the need to support the employee and the need to get the work done reliably and efficiently and to encourage the employee to understand that, even though their absences may all be entirely genuine, their level of attendance is still unsatisfactory from the employer's perspective and needs to improve. If the manager has reasonable grounds to believe that some or all of employee's absences are not genuine, the manager should put the available evidence to the employee at the meeting and seek a response.

Giving Formal Warnings for Unsatisfactory Attendance

As mentioned in the above section, it will be important for the manager to make the employee aware of the possible consequences of continuing unsatisfactory attendance.

If, following the review meeting, the employee's level of attendance remains at an unsatisfactory level, the manager should proceed, according to the employer's written procedures, to take formal action against the employee. This will usually take the form of a series of warnings (two, possibly three), leading eventually to dismissal if there is no improvement.

Such warnings will normally be for unsatisfactory attendance, and not for ill-health. This means that absences for reasons other than ill-health can be taken into account.

It is important also to distinguish between this type of warning and a disciplinary warning. Strictly speaking warnings for unsatisfactory attendance will not be disciplinary warnings, unless there is evidence to suggest that some of the employee's absences have not been for genuine reasons. Nevertheless, the procedure will be similar in its structure and operation to that used in cases of misconduct, but the terminology used should be different, as terms such as "misconduct" and "discipline" will be inappropriate.

Even where the reasons for an employee's absences are undisputedly genuine, this does not change the fact that the employee's work still needs to be done on a regular and reliable basis. If, therefore, the employee is not able to achieve such reliability, then warnings may be instigated. Moving to a process of formal warnings will be appropriate when the employee's absences have become excessive or where they are beginning to cause serious disruption, and where they have not improved following an earlier review meeting.

HOW TO PROCEED IF THERE IS EVIDENCE TO SUGGEST THAT AN EMPLOYEE'S ABSENCES ARE NOT GENUINE

In some cases it may be difficult to establish at the outset whether an employee's absences are due to:

● Genuine ill-health;

● Personal or family problems;

● Problems at work;

- No good reason, i.e. the employees has taken time off on the pretence of being sick.

If there is any doubt as to the root cause of the employee's frequent absences, the employee should, in the first instance, be given the benefit of the doubt, with the matter being dealt with as an ill-health issue.

Where there is evidence to suggest that an employee's absences are due to factors other than ill-health, for example if the employee is malingering, faking illness, or taking days off for no good reason, this can be regarded as misconduct, allowing the manager to deal with the matter under the employer's disciplinary procedure.

It will be important, however, before embarking on disciplinary procedures, to establish whether there is in fact evidence to lead to a conclusion that the employee's absences are not genuine. The manager should seek to establish this through investigation and consultation with the employee.

Care should be taken not to make assumptions or jump to unsubstantiated conclusions. For example if an employee telephones their manager in the morning stating that they have hurt their back and cannot walk and, later the same day, a colleague happens to see the same employee digging his garden, the manager may reasonably conclude that the employee's stated reason for absence is not genuine. If, on the other hand, the same employee is seen enjoying a pint of beer in a pub that evening, this does not necessarily mean that the employee was lying. An employee may well be capable of going out socially whilst genuinely unfit to perform their normal job duties.

Nevertheless, in circumstances such as these, the manager would be entitled to put the evidence they have to the employee at the return-to-work interview and invite the employee to comment. The matter should be dealt with factually, and not in a critical or accusatory manner. The manager should state simply that it was reported that the employee was seen in the pub/digging the garden at a particular time, and asked to comment on that in relation to the reason they gave for their absence. If the employee denies what has been reported, there may be nothing further the manager can do about it (unless proof of improper conduct is available), but at the very least the employee, if they were lying about the reason for their absence, will be alerted to the fact that the manager is "on to them".

FAMILY AND CHILDCARE PROBLEMS THAT CAUSE ABSENCE

Every employee who is a parent will inevitably experience occasions where time off work is unexpectedly required to deal with a child's sickness or other family crisis. Managers should exercise reasonable sympathy and tolerance towards employees who, for family reasons outside their control, need to take time off work.

Time off Work to Care for Dependants

Over and above this basic principle, there is a statutory duty on employers to grant employees reasonable time off work in certain defined circumstances involving a close dependant of the employee. The statutory right to time off work to care for dependants was introduced in December 1999 and provides for the following:

- All employees have the statutory right to take a reasonable amount of time off work to "care for dependants".

- There is no minimum service requirement for this right to be available.

- Such time off need not be paid, unless the employee's contract provides for paid time off for personal or family reasons, for example the contract might provide for a defined number of paid days off in the event of a family bereavement.

- A "dependant" is the spouse, civil partner, parent or child of the employee, or any other person who lives in the same household (excluding lodgers, tenants, boarders and employees). It also includes any other person who reasonably relies on the employee for their care, or for making arrangements for their care. This could include, for example an elderly neighbour who normally relies on the employee for their care.

The amount of time off that is "reasonable" is not defined in law, but the intention behind the legislation was that, in most cases, one or two days would be sufficient.

The circumstances in which an employee can take time off work are defined as follows:

- In the event that a dependant falls ill, is injured or assaulted;

- In the event of the death of a dependant;

- When a dependant gives birth;

- If there is disruption to the care arrangements of a dependant, for example where child-care arrangements have unexpectedly fallen through;

- Where an incident involving a child occurs unexpectedly at the child's school, requiring the immediate presence of the parent.

The purpose of these statutory provisions is to ensure that an employee who is facing some family emergency or unexpected problem involving a close family member can take a reasonable amount of time off work to deal with the problem. It is *not* the case that an employee has the right to claim unlimited time off work, nor can they claim time off in respect of an event that is planned, for example if their partner has arranged to go into hospital for an operation on a specific date.

Often, the amount of time off that the employee will be entitled to take will be only what is necessary to allow them to make the essential arrangements for the care of the dependant. For example, in *Forster v Cartwright Black Solicitors [2004] IRLR 781,* the EAT ruled that an employee who had taken several weeks off work on account of the emotional effects of having lost both her parents within four months of each other was not entitled to regard such leave as time off to care for dependants. The EAT stated that the right to time off in consequence of the death of a dependant is restricted to that which is necessary as a result of the death, for example taking care of necessary legal matters or arranging and attending the funeral.

There is also a duty in law for an employee to notify the employer of the reason for their absence as soon as is reasonably practicable.

In *Truelove v Safeway Stores plc [2005] ICR 589*, it was ruled that an employee whose childcare arrangements for the following day fell through late the previous day (and who notified the employer of this fact around 9.30 pm) had not acted in breach of the relevant statutory provisions when he took the day off despite having been refused permission to do so. The employee had indicated earlier in the day (around 4.00 pm) that there was a possibility that he might have to look after his child the following day and so, the EAT held, he had fulfilled his statutory duty to tell his employer about why he could not attend work the next day.

THE IMPORTANCE OF EXPLORING WHETHER AN EMPLOYEE'S ABSENCES MAY BE WORK-RELATED

If something in the workplace is causing or contributing to an employee's absences, it is obviously better for the manager to acknowledge the problem and take steps to remove or reduce it if possible. There are many aspects of work and many elements in the working environment that may cause an employee to take time off work on grounds of sickness absence, and there is much a manager can do to reduce the likelihood of such absences occurring.

Dealing with Workplace Stress

Recent research suggests that stress is one of the most important reasons behind absence from work and that stress-related absences are on the increase.

The CBI, for example, has estimated that at least one third of all employee sickness absence is due to mental ill-health. The Health and Safety Executive (HSE) has reported that:

- Stress is likely to become the most dangerous risk to business in the early years of the 21st century.

- One in five workers reports feeling extremely stressed at work. This equates to five million people in the UK.

- Self-reported work-related stress, depression or anxiety account for an estimated 10.5 million reported lost working days per year in Britain.

There is much that a manager can do to prevent, or at least reduce the likelihood of absences related to workplace stress. Stress – defined by the Health and Safety Executive as "the reaction people have to excessive pressures or other types of demand placed on them" is inherent to one degree or another in almost every job but can become a serious problem where pressures on individual employees are so great that they are no longer able to cope. Managers should bear in mind that every employee is different as regards how much or how little pressure they can effectively deal with. For example, one employee may cope extremely well with a very high volume of work, pressure from customers or tight deadlines whilst another may suffer symptoms of ill-health in exactly the same circumstances. That does not mean that one employee is strong and the other weak, it is simply that people are different in terms of their abilities to cope when work or factors in the workplace cause them stress.

Stress may be experienced as a result of an exposure to a wide range of work demands. Stress at work can also, in turn, contribute to an equally wide range of ill-health outcomes for the employee. Some of the workplace factors that can cause stress include:

- Excessive workloads;
- Targets and/or deadlines that are perceived as unachievable or unrealistic;
- Over-long working hours, eventually causing the employee to become exhausted;
- Lack of effective or meaningful communication in the workplace;
- Conflicting priorities;
- Lack of understanding and/or recognition;
- Lack of training or support;
- Worry over factors such as job security, change, etc;
- Bullying, harassment or conflict at work;
- Environmental factors.

Most employees will be able to cope with the above sorts of problems at work for a temporary period of time, but if the problem continues indefinitely with no indication that matters are likely to change for the better, then the employee may eventually experience a level of stress that they can no longer cope with. This situation, if not resolved, will eventually result in the employee going off sick, possibly for a short period of days or weeks, and sometimes for a much longer period of time. Such an outcome is in the interests of neither the employee nor the employer.

If, however, the cause of an employee's stress-related absences can be identified and removed, the employee's attendance may well improve. Managers may wish to bear in mind also that a failure on an employer's part to take reasonable steps to support an employee who is experiencing health problems as a result of factors in the workplace may lead the organisation to be held liable in law if the employee subsequently has a mental breakdown and if the breakdown was reasonably foreseeable.

A further problem is that many employees, understandably, may be reluctant to disclose to their manager that they feel stressed at work for fear that they will be perceived as weak or incompetent, out of embarrassment or feelings of guilt or even because of a perception that they might be dismissed for lack of capability. Thus the manager may only learn that an employee is suffering from workplace stress after they have been signed off sick by their doctor, by which time the damage has already been done.

Managers should therefore strive to eliminate or reduce the causes of employee stress if they wish to reduce and control employee absence. There are many courses of action that may be appropriate and these are listed below.

● Review employees' jobs and the methods of doing them, for example make sure that every employee has clearly defined job duties and objectives, make sure each employee knows how their job fits into the organisation as a whole, seek to cut out any unnecessary work or duplication of effort and review procedures to make sure they are operating efficiently.

- Make sure that no employee has an unreasonably high workload, unrealistic targets or over-tight deadlines that may cause an unacceptable level of stress.

- Check to see whether any employee is working excessively long hours, and if this is found to be the case, resolve to work with the employee to change this pattern so that they restrict their working hours to a reasonable level in the future and take proper breaks and holidays.

- Talk to individual employees about their jobs and their workloads in order to assess whether the demands being made on them are within that individual's coping resources.

- Consider introducing or extending flexible working practices such as part-time working, different shift patterns, flexi-time, etc, with the key aim being to offer employees a choice, if possible, as to their working pattern and number of hours.

- Examine whether effective two-way communication is taking place in the workplace, for example check to make sure (and do not assume) that employees are clear about what is expected of them in terms of work output, standards of work and priorities, provide regular feedback on performance, create opportunities for employees to contribute ideas and take positive steps to ensure employees are fully informed, involved and, if appropriate, consulted about matters that affect them.

- Make sure that every employee receives sufficient training, support and resources to perform their job, bearing in mind that individuals differ in terms of the amount of training and support they need.

- Take the time to communicate to employees that their skills and efforts are recognised and valued.

- Implement an anti-bullying/anti-harassment policy and make sure any complaints raised are always taken seriously and dealt with promptly, objectively and fairly.

One of the common threads running through cases of work-related stress is that the employee will feel out of control in terms of performing their job or coping with the workload. It follows that, if the manager can delegate more autonomy to individual employees as to how they perform their jobs or at least consult them about the matters noted above, this may help to reduce workplace stress.

It is advisable for managers always to be vigilant to the possibility of workplace stress, and to adopt a positive attitude to reducing and resolving the possible causes. Managers who think that this problem does not apply to them or their departments should bear in mind that, just because no one has complained, this does not mean that the problem of workplace stress does not exist. As stated earlier, few employees will admit to stress until forced to do so after their health has already been adversely affected.

WHEN DISMISSAL ON ACCOUNT OF FREQUENT ABSENTEEISM MAY BE FAIR

As is the case for long-term sickness absence, there is no defined time limit in law as to what level of absenteeism may, ultimately, justify dismissal. Whether a particular employee's level of absenteeism is sufficient to justify a dismissal will inevitably depend on a number of factors, including:

- The frequency and total length of the employee's absences;

- The reasons for the absences;

- The likelihood of the employee's absence pattern continuing in the future;

- The effect of the employee's absences on colleagues and on the business;

- The size and resources of the employer;

- The feasibility of employing a temporary replacement each time the employee is absent.

The key question relevant to whether or not an employer will have proper grounds for dismissing an employee for unsatisfactory attendance is whether in all the circumstances, the employer can reasonably be expected to wait any longer for the employee to be fit to attend work on a regular and reliable basis. Employers are not expected to tolerate an employee's frequent absences indefinitely.

Before taking any decision to dismiss, the manager must make sure that they have:

- Conducted a fair review of the employee's attendance record, and the reasons for the frequent absences;

- Issued the employee with an appropriate number of warnings (a minimum of two) saying that a continuing unsatisfactory level of attendance would lead to dismissal;

- Afforded the employee a fair opportunity to put forward representations at an properly convened and conducted formal interview.

In *Lynock v Cereal Packaging Ltd [1988] IRLR 510*, the EAT issued useful guidance as to the factors that would be relevant in determining whether or not a decision to dismiss an employee on the grounds of absence was fair:

- The nature of the employee's illnesses;

- The likelihood of illness recurring or some other illness arising;

- The length of the various absences and the periods of good health between them;

- The employer's need for the work to be done by the particular employee;

- The impact of the absences on the employee's colleagues;

- The adoption and the implementation of a sickness absence policy;

- A personal assessment of the situation before the ultimate decision to dismiss was taken;

- The extent to which the difficulty of the situation and the position of the employer had been made clear to the employee so that the employee realised the ultimate decision-making moment was approaching.

The EAT also said that in cases involving sickness absences, the employer's approach should be based on "sympathy, understanding and compassion".

KEY POINTS

The manager should:

- Instigate an absence management procedure as soon as an employee phones in sick.

- Adopt a stringent return-to-work interview process so that each time an employee returns to work after an absence, the absence is discussed directly with them and recorded.

- Make sure employees always complete a self-certification form for all periods of sickness absence of less than one working week and that the form is signed by both the employee and the manager.

- Set up a review meeting with any employee whose level of absenteeism has reached an unacceptable level.

- Examine the employee's absence record to see whether there is any pattern to the absences, and if so prepare to put this observation to the employee at the review meeting.

- Aim during the review meeting to investigate whether there is any underlying cause of the employee's frequent absences and to make the employee aware that their level of attendance has reached a level that is unacceptable.

- Recognise that there are many potential underlying causes for frequent, persistent absences, some of which may be linked to factors in the workplace.

- Adopt a supportive approach towards any employee who has had a high level of absenteeism.

- Set reasonable targets and time limits for improvement in the employee's level of attendance and seek to gain the employee's commitment to try to achieve such improvement.

- Make sure the employee understands what the consequences will be of a failure to achieve a satisfactory level of attendance, i.e. formal action may follow with a series of warnings and eventual dismissal.

- Aim to strike a balance between the need to support the employee and the need to get the work done reliably and efficiently.

- Move to a process of formal warnings if an employee's absences have become excessive or where they are beginning to cause serious disruption, and where attendance has not improved following an earlier review meeting.

- Refrain from making assumptions or jumping to unsubstantiated conclusions that an employee's absences are not for genuine reasons.

- Exercise reasonable sympathy and tolerance towards employees who, for family reasons outside their control, need to take time off work.

- Recognise the statutory duty on employers to grant employees reasonable time off work in certain defined circumstances involving their close dependants.

- Acknowledge that there is a great deal that a manager can do to prevent or at least reduce the likelihood of stress-related absences.

- Be vigilant to the possibility of workplace stress, and adopt a positive attitude to reducing and resolving its possible causes.

- Before taking any decision to dismiss an employee for absenteeism, make sure that there has been a fair review of the employee's attendance record, that the employee has had the appropriate number of warnings and that the employee has been afforded a fair opportunity to put forward representations at a properly convened and conducted interview.

CHAPTER 8
DISMISSALS AND GENERAL CRITERIA FOR FAIRNESS

INTRODUCTION

This chapter aims to provide the reader with a summary of the laws regulating dismissal, and to add to the information already provided in the preceding chapters on the appropriate procedures to be followed in the event of misconduct, unsatisfactory performance, long-term ill-health absence and persistent absenteeism. The approach used by employment tribunals when addressing claims of unfair dismissal and the remedies that they may order, are also discussed, as is the subject of notice periods.

AN EMPLOYEE'S STATUTORY RIGHT NOT TO BE UNFAIRLY DISMISSED

Most employees are eligible to bring a claim for unfair dismissal before an employment tribunal. The conditions for eligibility are that:

- The person must have been an employee of the organisation – freelance workers, sub-contractors, agency staff and self-employed people are therefore not eligible.

- The employee must not work wholly outside Britain (but see below).

- The employee must have attained a minimum of one year's continuous service prior to their date of termination.

Part-time employees are protected by the unfair dismissal legislation in the same way as full-time employees, irrespective of the number of hours they work per week or month. Temporary employees are similarly eligible provided they have the requisite one-year's continuous service (which could be on a single contract or a series of consecutive short contracts with no gaps between them).

There is no lower or upper age limit on the right to claim unfair dismissal.

There are a number of exceptions to the rule that requires an employee to have a minimum of one year's service in order to qualify for the right to claim unfair dismissal. These include any dismissal that is discriminatory on the grounds of sex, race, religion or belief, sexual orientation, age or disability or on grounds that the individual has exercised or asserted one of a range of statutory rights (see also below under "Dismissals that are Automatically Unfair").

Employees Working Outside Britain

Normally, an employee who works wholly outside Britain will be unable, in the event of dismissal, to bring a claim for unfair dismissal to a UK employment tribunal. However, since the 2006 judgement in the conjoined cases of *Lawson v Serco Ltd; Botham v Ministry of Defence; Crofts & ors v Veta [2006] UKHL 3,* some expatriate employees may be eligible to bring claims of unfair dismissal despite working wholly overseas. The House of Lords held that in the circumstances below, an expatriate employee might be deemed to be "employed in Great Britain":

- where the employee had been posted abroad by a British employer "for the purposes of a business carried on in Britain" (i.e. the work the employee performed overseas was for a business based in Britain);

- where the employee was working for a British overseas territory or a political or social British enclave (which was the situation in the *Lawson* and *Botham* cases).

Additionally, the House of Lords ruled that a peripatetic employee based in the UK but whose work involved worldwide travel might be deemed to be employed in Great Britain if their "home base" for employment purposes was located in Britain. These were the circumstances in the *Crofts* case which concerned a pilot working for an overseas airline but functionally based at Heathrow airport.

Another point to note is that foreign nationals working in Britain, whether permanently or temporarily and whether employed by a UK company or one based overseas, are protected by the unfair dismissal provisions in the same way as UK nationals.

Time Limits for Bringing a Claim

The standard time period within which a dismissed employee must lodge their unfair dismissal claim with the Office of Employment Tribunals is three calendar months, effective from the date of the termination of the contract of employment. The tribunal does have discretion, however, to extend this time limit if, in their reasoned opinion, it was not reasonably practicable for the claimant to lodge the claim in time. Otherwise, a claim will be "out of time" which will usually result in the dismissed employee losing their right to have the complaint heard.

WHAT IS A DISMISSAL?

A dismissal is defined in law as:

- the termination by an employer of the contract under which an employee is employed;

- the expiry of a fixed-term contract without renewal;

- the resignation by an employee (with or without notice) in circumstances where the employee is entitled to terminate the contract by reason of the employer's breach of contract (known as constructive dismissal – see chapter 9).

In most cases of termination, it is clear whether it is the employer or the employee who has instigated or caused the termination. In a few cases, however, there may be doubt.

The "Resign or be Fired" Approach

If an employee is pressurised into resigning (with or without threatening tactics), or openly threatened with dismissal if they decline to resign, this will be regarded in law as an express dismissal. The reasoning behind this concept is straightforward. A logical analysis would make it clear that the termination of the employee's contract had been caused by the employer and not as a result of the employee choosing to leave. In other words, the employee is left with no choice as to whether or not to remain in their employment. The only choice they have is in the means used to terminate the contract, i.e. whether they resign or are fired. Either way, the employment will come to an end.

Inducing an Employee to Resign and/or Offering an Exit Package

Whilst the "resign or be fired" approach is usually easy to identify as a dismissal, it may be less clear whether "gentle persuasion" to resign carries the same status.

In the case of *Billington v Michael Hunter and Sons Ltd EAT [2003] 0578/03,* an employee, who had received a formal written warning following a number of complaints about her from customers, was told by her manager that if there were any further complaints, she "would very likely be dismissed". The manager then told her (in a calm and measured way) that if she were to decide that the job was beyond her capabilities, she could resign "on favourable terms". The manager added that he hoped her performance would improve, and that dismissal would not be necessary. The employee subsequently did resign, but not on the favourable terms that had been hinted at. Instead she brought a claim for constructive dismissal to tribunal, asserting that the employer had breached the implied term of trust and confidence that is inherent in every contract of employment.

The EAT agreed with the employee that the manager's invitation to resign coupled with the earlier warning and the statement that further incidents would lead to dismissal was behaviour that was likely to destroy or seriously damage the working relationship. This was to be regarded as a fundamental breach of contract, entitling the employee to resign and claim constructive dismissal.

This case essentially means that if an employee is offered an "exit package" (however attractive) as an alternative to going through formal disciplinary or capability procedures (where dismissal is by no means certain), this may constitute grounds for the employee to resign and claim constructive dismissal. On the other hand, if the employee chooses to accept the package on offer, all will be well (but see below under "Compromise agreements").

EMPLOYERS' OPTIONS WHEN FACING A CLAIM FOR UNFAIR DISMISSAL

If a dismissed employee has lodged a claim for unfair dismissal, or if the employer fears that they might do so, various options are open to the employer to deal with the situation:

- Defend the claim at a tribunal hearing;

- Seek to settle the claim through ACAS conciliation before the hearing date;

- Negotiate a compromise agreement to settle the claim;

- Reach a private agreement to settle the claim and ask the tribunal to validate it;

- Seek to agree with the employee to submit the claim to ACAS arbitration.

In practice, most employers facing a potential claim for unfair dismissal choose to settle the claim before a tribunal hearing in order to minimise cost, management time, stress, disruption to the business and the risk of adverse publicity. Employers are, however, under no legal obligation to negotiate or accept an offer of settlement.

ACAS Conciliation

Each time a tribunal claim is lodged, an ACAS conciliation officer is routinely notified. One of the functions of ACAS (the Advisory, Conciliation and Arbitration Service) is to assist employers and employees to resolve any dispute that they may have.

Once a claim is lodged therefore, the employer will be contacted by an ACAS conciliation officer to see whether there is a possibility of a settlement. If the dismissed employee wishes it and if it is thought practicable, the conciliation officer will seek to promote their reinstatement or re-engagement. Otherwise, they will seek to promote agreement between the parties as to a sum of money by way of compensation. The conciliation officer will not give advice as to the merits or demerits of the employee's claim, nor recommend what form a settlement should take, but will be able to act as an impartial intermediary to facilitate communication between the parties. It is recommended that managers should be willing to cooperate with the conciliation officer, as they may often be able to help to identify a solution that will bring the matter to a conclusion.

The employer is under no legal duty to reach a settlement through ACAS conciliation, but it is often advisable to do so, particularly if by that point in time it has been realised that the dismissal may have been unfair, perhaps in respect of a flaw in the carrying out of the relevant procedures. A settlement, once reached, is usually recorded on a form known as a COT3, and is binding to prevent the employee proceeding further with the claim.

Compromise Agreements

Employers may sometimes prefer to negotiate with an employee whom they wish to dismiss in order to reach a private termination agreement, rather than go ahead with the dismissal and risk facing a complaint of unfair dismissal being brought to an employment tribunal. If this process is to be legally binding, it must be achieved through a "compromise agreement", which, if properly drafted, can act to prevent the employee from taking a particular complaint to a court or employment tribunal, or continuing with the complaint (if it has already been lodged).

A compromise agreement may be reached either before or after the commencement of tribunal proceedings. There are no time limits or fixed periods within which an agreement may be instigated or concluded. In order for a compromise agreement to be binding, however, the following conditions must be met:

- The agreement must be in writing;

- The agreement must relate to the specific complaint in question (i.e. be drafted to identify unfair dismissal as the specific complaint, rather than worded in a generalised way in an attempt to compromise all types of claim);

- The employee must have received advice from a relevant independent advisor (usually a lawyer) as to the terms and effect of the proposed agreement;

- The agreement must identify the advisor who must, at the relevant time, have insurance or an indemnity covering the risk of a claim against them;

- The agreement must state that the conditions regulating compromise agreements have been satisfied.

A failure to comply with any one of these statutory requirements will have the effect of rendering the agreement unenforceable.

The advisor engaged for the purpose of giving the employee advice must be an independent advisor (and not, for example, the employer's in-house lawyer). As well as qualified lawyers, trade union officials certified by the union as competent to give advice and certified advisors working on an unpaid basis at advice centres will qualify as independent advisors for this purpose.

The advisor's role is to explain the terms of the proposed agreement fully to the employee, and in particular to make them aware that signing the agreement will prevent them from taking or continuing proceedings before an employment tribunal.

Employers cannot of course force any employee to enter into a compromise agreement. It will be up to the manager dealing with the case to negotiate with the employee and/or their representative or lawyer as to the financial aspect of the settlement. It is usually advisable to ask for a confidentiality clause as part of the agreement.

Private Settlements

Managers should note that any termination agreement reached privately between the parties that does not meet the stringent requirements of a compromise agreement will not be legally binding to prevent the employee taking their claim of unfair dismissal to tribunal (but see also next section). This is the case even where the employee has signed such an agreement. Whatever level of skills a particular manager may believe they possess in drafting contractual documents, any such document produced by the manager will not be worth the paper it is written on, as it will not be capable of acting to prevent the employee from taking the claim to tribunal. The right to claim unfair dismissal is a statutory right for all employees (subject to the eligibility conditions identified above) and this right cannot be overridden or contracted out of by the employer.

Tribunal Validation of a Settlement

Notwithstanding the fact that a private agreement to settle a dispute will not, on its own, be legally binding to prevent the employee proceeding to take their unfair dismissal claim to tribunal, the employer and the employee may reach a private agreement and then ask the employment tribunal (at the hearing) to validate it.

In these circumstances, the tribunal will usually make an order dismissing the proceedings by consent on the basis that the claimant is withdrawing their claim, with terms of settlement having been agreed. This will have the effect of preventing the claimant from continuing or recommencing proceedings in respect of the same complaint.

The ACAS Arbitration Scheme

An alternative method of dealing with unfair dismissal claims is available through ACAS arbitration. The scheme is a voluntary arbitration scheme dealing with straightforward cases of unfair dismissal (rather than those that include complexities such as whether or not the claimant is eligible in the first place to bring the claim). Once the employee has agreed to submit to ACAS arbitration, they will, in effect, have signed away their right to pursue the claim through an employment tribunal as it will be dealt with at an ACAS hearing instead.

To use the scheme, both the employer and the employee must agree voluntarily to enter into arbitration with an ACAS appointed arbitrator, and agree to be bound by the decision. There is no right of appeal against the decision. The process is less formal than the procedures adopted by employment tribunals and may have a number of advantages such as:

- Confidentiality – decisions are not reported;

- Quicker – the fact there is no right of appeal means that the case will be concluded within a reasonably short time-scale thus giving certainty to both parties;

- Less legalistic;

- Less stressful due to the more informal processes at the hearing, for example both parties are simply invited to state their cases and there is no cross-examination of witnesses.

The ACAS arbitrator has the same powers as an employment tribunal to award reinstatement, re-engagement or compensation if the case succeeds (see below).

THE CRITERIA FOR A DISMISSAL TO BE FAIR

There are a number of elements relevant to the question of the fairness of a dismissal. These are:

- The reason for the dismissal, and whether it is one of the reasons permitted by legislation;

- Whether the reason is sufficient to justify dismissal (the "sufficiency test");

- Whether the employer has (in a general sense) acted reasonably in dismissing the employee for the stated reason; *and*

- Whether the employer has adhered to its own internal procedures.

An employer tribunal will also consider whether the employer has adhered to the guidance given in the ACAS Code of Practice on Disciplinary and Grievance Procedures.

These issues are each explored more fully below.

Thus the fact that an employer has a solid reason to dismiss an employee is not sufficient, on its own, to ensure fairness. It is imperative also to ensure that proper procedures are followed, otherwise the dismissal will be unfair irrespective of the seriousness or genuineness of the circumstances that led to the employee's dismissal.

This concept can, understandably, appear strange to managers who are unfamiliar with unfair dismissal law. For example, an employee who is caught stealing from their employer and consequently dismissed for that reason may, despite proof of the thefts being available, go on to win a claim for unfair dismissal at an employment tribunal on the grounds that the employer failed to adhere to correct procedures.

It may be easier to understand the logic of this by looking at the function of an employment tribunal. A tribunal's function is not to judge whether an employee is guilty of misconduct, but rather to assess whether the conduct of the employer was fair and reasonable in light of all the circumstances. The consideration of whether or not the employee is guilty of misconduct will be relevant, but only to the extent that it may influence the level of any compensation awarded if the case is upheld. The basic decision as to whether or not the dismissal was fair will depend not only on the employer's reason for dismissing the employee, but on procedural factors as well. The tribunal, in order to reach a decision, must:

- Consider all the relevant circumstances of the case;

- Weigh up all the evidence;

- Make findings of fact (which in cases where the facts are disputed will involve deciding objectively whose evidence is to be believed);

- Act objectively in assessing the way in which the employer has dealt with the dismissal;

- Interpret the law and not substitute their own views about the employer's reason for dismissal or whether it was sufficient to justify the penalty of dismissal.

In summary, if an employer is to succeed in defending a claim for unfair dismissal at a tribunal hearing, they must first be able to show a fair and sufficient reason for the dismissal and then they must also be able to demonstrate to the tribunal's satisfaction that they followed fair procedures and acted reasonably in the manner in which they carried out the dismissal.

Potentially Fair Reasons for Dismissal

The first task for the employer who wishes to defend a claim for unfair dismissal at a tribunal hearing will be to establish, to the tribunal's satisfaction, the reason for the dismissal. The burden of proof is on the employer to achieve this, although it is not usually difficult to do so. Absolute proof beyond reasonable doubt is not required as employment tribunal's work to the "balance of probabilities' test".

The reason for dismissal must fall within one of the potentially fair reasons listed in the *Employment Rights Act 1996*. These are:

- Capability

- Conduct

- Redundancy

- Retirement

- Legal restriction

- Some other substantial reason (SOSR).

The categories of "retirement", "legal restriction" and "some other substantial reason" are discussed in chapter 9. Conduct is covered fully in chapters 2, 3 and 4, whilst capability issues (unsatisfactory job performance and ill-health) are dealt with in chapters 5, 6 and 7. Redundancy dismissals are outside the scope of this book.

If the employer is unable to show the reason for the employee's dismissal, or if the reason stated is not one of the list of potentially fair reasons, the dismissal will be unfair. Similarly if the employer presents a reason for dismissal without any evidence to substantiate it, or if the evidence suggests that there was in reality a completely different reason for the dismissal, then the dismissal will be unfair.

The "Sufficiency Test"

Whatever the reason given for an employee's dismissal, it must be sufficient to justify dismissal. For example, if an employee has been dismissed for stealing, the question would arise as to what precise form the misconduct took. If the reason for dismissal was that the employee on one occasion stole a pencil out of the employer's stationery cupboard and took it home for personal use, this would be unlikely to be sufficient to justify the penalty of dismissal. If, however, the employer had previously warned the employee in writing that taking items out of the stationery cupboard home for personal use would lead to their dismissal, or if a well-communicated policy or rule clearly identified such conduct as gross misconduct, then the outcome could be different, i.e. the dismissal could, in theory, be fair. The same principle would apply to dismissals for unsatisfactory performance – one mistake would not normally be sufficient to justify a dismissal (unless it amounted to gross negligence or had very serious consequences), whilst a dismissal following a series of warnings about continuing mistakes might very well be considered fair.

Managers, when considering dismissing an employee, should take care not to let emotions such as anger and impatience cloud their judgement as to whether an employee's behaviour is – when viewed objectively – sufficient to justify the penalty of dismissal.

The General Principle of Reasonableness

Employment tribunals are under a duty to consider whether the employer acted reasonably in dismissing the employee, taking into account all the circumstances of the particular case. This means that the tribunal will assess whether or not the manner in which the employer carried out the dismissal fell within what is commonly known as the "band of reasonable responses" which an employer might have adopted. The burden of proof is neutral in this respect.

The concept of reasonableness has developed extensively over the years through case law. In the landmark case of *Polkey v A E Dayton Services Ltd [1987] IRLR 503,* the House of Lords provided some useful general guidelines as to the procedural steps that would be necessary if a dismissal was to be found fair:

● In a case of incapacity, the employer would have to give the employee fair warning and a chance to improve;

- In a case of misconduct, the employer would have to investigate fully and fairly and hear what the employee had to say in explanation or mitigation;

- In a case of redundancy, the employer would have to warn and consult affected employees, adopt a fair basis for selection and take reasonable steps to re-deploy affected employees.

If an employer had a sound reason for dismissing an employee, but the dismissal was nevertheless found to be unfair on the basis of procedural shortcomings, the employee's compensation is normally reduced by the tribunal to take into account the fact that the employee's conduct caused or contributed to their dismissal.

Adhering to Internal Procedures

Following procedures is a vital element in fairness whenever dismissal is being contemplated. Managers should, without exception, always follow the organisation's own internal disciplinary procedures when taking steps to dismiss an employee, whether for misconduct or lack of capability. A failure to do so is likely to render the dismissal unfair.

Misconduct as a Reason for Dismissal

Misconduct is, ultimately, a potentially fair reason for dismissal, provided:

- The employee's misconduct was the real reason for the dismissal;

- The employer genuinely believed, at the time of the dismissal, that the employee committed the act of misconduct in question and that the circumstances justified dismissal;

- This belief was based on reasonable grounds;

- In all the circumstances of the case (including the size and resources of the employer), the employer acted reasonably in dismissing the employee for the specific reason given;

- The employer had carried out a full and fair investigation into the alleged misconduct;

- The employer followed a fair and reasonable procedure prior to taking the decision to dismiss, including holding an interview with the employee to establish their version of events and allowing a right of appeal.

Employment tribunals do not require employers to show that they had proof beyond reasonable doubt of the employee's misconduct. Instead, the decision is made using the "balance of probabilities test". In cases of misconduct, the tribunal will look for evidence that the employer held a genuine belief, based on reasonable grounds, after a thorough investigation, that there was sufficient reason to dismiss based on the facts known to them at the time. These principles emanate from the case of *British Home Stores Ltd v Burchell [1978] IRLR 379* (see chapter 4, "The three-part test for fairness").

Capability as a Reason for Dismissal

"Capability" is defined in law as the employee's "skill, qualifications, aptitude, health or any other physical or mental quality". The most common issues that arise are unsatisfactory job performance due to lack of skill and ill-health causing absence from work.

Unsatisfactory job performance

In order for an employer to show that a dismissal for unsatisfactory performance was fair on the grounds of capability, the employee's lack of capability must relate to the type of work they were employed to do. This in turn will depend on the terms of the employee's contract and the duties and responsibilities laid down in their job description, if there is one. If the employee's failure to perform to the required standard was in relation to duties that fell outside their contractual duties, the employer would be unable to establish that their inability to perform those duties was a fair reason for dismissal.

The employer would have to show that:

- The real reason for dismissal was the employee's unsatisfactory performance and that specific evidence of unsatisfactory performance was available (the manager's opinion of the employee's performance would not, on its own, be enough);

- In all the circumstances of the case (including the size and resources of the employer), the employer acted reasonably in dismissing the employee;

- The employee had been given a full opportunity to improve to the standard reasonably required for effective performance of the job and sufficient training and time to improve to that standard;

- The employee had been given fair warning that continuing unsatisfactory performance would lead to dismissal and a proper opportunity to put forward their side of things;

- The dismissal was procedurally fair, for example an interview with the employee was held prior to the decision to dismiss being taken and a right of appeal was granted.

Ill-health

For the purposes of unfair dismissal legislation, cases of ill health also fall under the category of "capability". Clearly if an employee is ill, suffering from a physical or mental condition that adversely affects work performance, or is absent from work due to sickness or injury, then they are "incapable" of performing their duties. A dismissal on the grounds of genuine ill-health can be fair in law provided proper procedures are followed.

There is no guidance in law as to the time period after which it may be fair to dismiss an employee who is absent from work due to ill-health. The key question that determines fairness (or unfairness) in a dismissal for ill-health, is whether in all the circumstances the employer can reasonably be expected, in light of their business requirements, to wait any longer for the employee to recover and attend work on a regular and reliable basis.

Before contemplating termination of an employee's employment on grounds of long-term ill-health, however, the manager should be looking at ways of facilitating the employee's return to work. This issue is discussed fully in chapter 6.

For a dismissal on the grounds of ill-health to be fair, the employer would have to show that:

161

- Lack of capability caused by ill-health and/or absence from work was the real reason for dismissal;

- In all the circumstances of the case (including the size and resources of the employer), the employer acted reasonably in dismissing the employee for the reason given;

- The employer had waited a reasonable length of time before instituting steps to dismiss the employee;

- The employer had taken sufficient steps to obtain and interpret up-to-date medical evidence about the employee's fitness to work;

- The employee had been given fair warning that continuing absence from work would lead to dismissal and the opportunity to make representations;

- The dismissal was procedurally fair, for example the employee was afforded the opportunity of an interview prior to the decision to dismiss being taken and granted the right of appeal.

DISMISSALS THAT ARE AUTOMATICALLY UNFAIR

There is a long list of grounds for dismissal that are regarded in law as being automatically unfair. This means that, irrespective of whether the employer has followed proper procedures in the run up to the employee's dismissal, the dismissal will be ruled unfair if it is on one of the prohibited grounds. Furthermore, in most (but not all) cases, the employee will not need to have the usual one year's qualifying service in order to bring the claim to tribunal. The list includes dismissal:

- In connection with the statutory right to be accompanied at disciplinary and grievance hearings by a colleague of the employee's choice or a trade union representative (see chapter 2);

- Because the employee has taken time off work, or applied to do so, on account of being called up for jury service;

- For any reason relating to pregnancy, maternity leave or childbirth;

- For a reason related to other family leave (paternity, adoption or parental leave or time off work to care for dependants – see the *Palen* case below);

- In connection with the right to request flexible working (which is available to employees with a minimum of six months' continuous service who have parental responsibility for a child under six years old or caring responsibilities for a dependant adult);

- Because an employee who is a protected or opted-out shop or betting worker has refused to work on Sundays;

- Of an occupational pension scheme trustee because they have carried out the functions of this post;

- Of an employee representative in connection with their duties in that capacity;

- In connection with information and consultation rights under the *Information and Consultation of Employees Regulations 2004*;

- Because the employee has carried out the functions of a member of a European Works Council, taken part in associated activities or requested or taken time off work to perform such functions or take part in such activities;

- For making a protected disclosure under the *Public Interest Disclosure Act 1998*;

- For asserting one of a range of statutory rights;

- In connection with the entitlement to paid annual leave and other rights available to all workers under the *Working Time Regulations 1998*;

- In connection with entitlement to the national minimum wage;

- For a reason connected to working tax credits to which the employee is or may be entitled;

- On account of a "spent" conviction within the terms of the *Rehabilitation of Offenders Act 1974*, unless the employee's job falls into a category excluded from the provisions of that Act;

- In connection with trade union membership, activities or use of union services or an application or campaign for trade union recognition;

- For taking official industrial action in certain circumstances that render such action "protected";

- For a reason related to the fact that the employee is a health and safety representative, has participated in health and safety activities or has taken action for a reason related to health and safety;

- Where there is a transfer of an undertaking and the transfer, or a reason connected with it, is the reason or principal reason for the employee's dismissal (unless it is an "ETO" reason, which means an economic, technical or organisational reason entailing changes in the workforce, in which case the dismissal may be fair);

- In connection with the rights of part-time workers under the *Part-time Workers (Prevention of Less Favourable Treatment) Regulations 2000* or the rights of fixed-term employees under the *Fixed-term Employees (Prevention of Less Favourable Treatment) Regulations 2002*.

In *RKS Services v Palen [2007] EAT 0030/06*, the employee, a delivery driver in a small company, took a day off work during his second week of employment in order to care for his partner who had been taken ill. On his return to work, his manager told him that a small company could not afford to let people take time off in that way, and dismissed him. He brought a claim to tribunal asserting that the reason for his dismissal was that he had taken "time off to care for dependants", one of the prohibited reasons for dismissal. A claim of this type does not require any minimum period of service.

Although the employer asserted that the reason for the dismissal was that the employee had damaged a delivery van, the tribunal did not believe this and ruled that the reason for the dismissal was that the employee had taken a day off to care for his partner (which he was entitled to do in law). The tribunal therefore ruled that the dismissal was automatically unfair and this was upheld on appeal.

This case demonstrates the dangers of assuming that, because an employee has not yet gained a year's continuous service, they can be dismissed without any fear of legal repercussions.

NOTICE PERIODS

Where either an employer or an employee wishes to terminate a contract of employment, they must by law give the other party a minimum period of statutory notice, provided the employee has worked for the employer for at least one month. The only occasion when it is lawful for an employer to terminate an employee's contract without notice or pay in lieu of notice is in circumstances where the employee has committed an act of gross misconduct (see chapter 4) that justifies immediate dismissal.

Minimum Periods of Notice on Dismissal

Employers are under a duty to specify, as part of each employee's written particulars of employment, particulars of the length of notice that an employee is obliged to give and entitled to receive. Minimum periods of notice are prescribed by statute for both employee and employer. In essence, employees (if dismissed) are entitled, once they have at least one month's service, to a minimum of one week's notice for each completed year of service up to a maximum of 12 weeks.

Employers may, if they wish, choose to institute longer periods of notice under the contract of employment. Where this is done, the longer contractual notice periods will be enforceable. An employer may not, however, specify periods of notice that are shorter than those defined in statute. If they do so (perhaps as an oversight), the relevant statutory notice period will take precedence, thus guaranteeing the employee at least the minimum period of notice available to them by law.

Where an employer gives an employee insufficient notice of termination, or no notice at all, the employee will be entitled to add the relevant period of statutory notice to their length of service for the purposes of any statutory claim to an employment tribunal. This provision is important because it may influence the question of whether the employee has the requisite one-year's service to claim unfair dismissal or the two years' service necessary to claim a statutory redundancy payment. It may also be relevant to the determination of compensation if a claim succeeds, as the basic award for unfair dismissal is dependent (amongst other things) on the employee's length of service (see below).

Irrespective of what the contract of employment says, it is of course permissible for an employee and their manager to agree mutually at the time of proposed termination to a notice period that is shorter than the period defined in statute, or to waive the notice period altogether.

Common Law Notice

Under common law, an employee whose contract is terminated by the employer is entitled to a "reasonable" period of notice. This means that in certain circumstances, the notice period to which the employee is entitled could be longer than the relevant period of statutory notice. This could occur, for example, where an employee was engaged in a senior position in an organisation in which it was customary for a lengthy period of notice to be given. Similarly, if an employer had failed to define any notice periods under the employee's contract, a tribunal could, if the matter was challenged, decide ultimately that the applicable period of notice should be longer than the statutory period, depending on what they regarded as appropriate and reasonable in the particular circumstances.

Withdrawing or Varying Notice

There is no right in law for either the employer or the employee to withdraw notice to terminate a contract of employment once it has been given. This means that where an employee has been dismissed with notice by the employer, and where during the notice period the manager changes their mind about dismissing the employee, the employee is not obliged to agree to the withdrawal of the notice and the dismissal will therefore stand. There is, however, nothing to prevent the manager and the employee from reaching a mutual agreement to forget about the notice and continue the employment relationship on either the same or revised terms. The same principle applies in reverse, i.e. where the employee resigns but subsequently changes their mind about leaving, the manager will not be under any duty to agree to allow the employee to withdraw their notice.

Similarly, once the employer has given notice to terminate the contract, the notice period can only be extended or shortened where both parties agree to the change. This means that a manager cannot compel an employee to work longer than the notice provided for in statute or under their contract of employment, nor are they entitled to shorten the notice period against the employee's will, unless the employee is paid for the outstanding portion of the notice period (see next section). Unilaterally shortening the employee's period of notice without pay in lieu would in all probability have the effect of converting a resignation into a dismissal, which would almost certainly be unfair in law.

Pay in Lieu of Notice

Payment in lieu of notice may be made by the employer upon termination of the contract by either party. Where payment in lieu of notice is made, it must (unless the contract provides otherwise) be of a sufficient level to cover not only the employee's normal wages or salary, but also the value of any benefits that form part of the employee's contract, for example the value of the use of a company car, for the length of the notice period. Where pay in lieu of notice is made, the employee's contract will come to an end with immediate effect, rather than at the end of what would otherwise have been the notice period. This contrasts with the position in respect of "garden leave" – see below.

It is in the interests of the employer to ensure that each employee's contract includes a clause giving the employer the authority to elect, at their discretion, to grant pay in lieu of notice rather than permitting the employee to work out their notice period. This will mean that terminating with pay in lieu of notice will not constitute a breach of contract. Unfortunately, making this option a condition of the contract is not so advantageous for the employee, because where pay in lieu of notice is authorised by the contract, it is deemed to equate to salary/wages, which in turn means that it is taxable.

If, however, the contract does not expressly state that the employer may opt for pay in lieu of notice instead of notice itself, making a payment in lieu of notice technically amounts to a breach of contract. Although the dismissed employee would not stand to gain anything financially from this state of affairs, the effect of a dismissal in breach of contract (known as "wrongful dismissal") will be that none of the other clauses in the contract can subsequently be enforced.

This will be important if the contract contains provisions that are specifically set up to come into play after the employee's termination, for example a restrictive covenant designed to prevent the employee from working for a competitor or soliciting the employer's customers for a defined period after the end of employment, or a requirement for an employee to repay a loan or relocation expenses. In the event of a wrongful dismissal, because the employee is freed from all outstanding contractual obligations, the employer would be unable to enforce these contractual clauses through the courts.

Garden Leave

An alternative to allowing an employee to work throughout the notice period or making a payment in lieu of notice, is to place the employee on what is affectionately known as "garden leave". Garden leave is, in essence, paid leave of absence during which the employee, whilst not working, continues to be employed and thus remains bound by all the terms of their contract of employment. The only difference is that the employee is at home (presumably tending the garden!) instead of going in to work. Garden leave is often implemented by employers who wish to remove an employee from access to computers and/or confidential information and/or prevent them from joining a competitor for the duration of the notice period. Garden leave clauses are lawful provided the employee is given full pay and benefits up until the end of the notice period and provided the employee's level of pay does not depend on the provision of work.

Because an employee's contract of employment continues in force during garden leave, the date of termination does not occur until the end of the notice period.

The Importance of Being Clear about the Employee's Termination Date

It is important for both the employer and the employee to be clear about the date on which employment ends. This is principally because if the employee subsequently brings a claim for unfair dismissal to tribunal it may otherwise be disputed as to whether they have attained the necessary one year's qualifying service for the right to bring the claim, or whether they have lodged their claim within the relevant statutory time period (three months from the date of termination - see above).

Furthermore, both the employer and the employee will need to be clear for obvious reasons as to when contractual company benefits such as life insurance, medical insurance and pension benefits, are to terminate.

To avoid problems, employers should ensure that whenever an employee is dismissed, the termination date is unequivocally stated in writing and the employee clearly informed that all obligations and entitlements under the contract will cease on that date.

WRITTEN REASONS FOR DISMISSAL

Employees who have at least one year's continuous service have the right, on request, to receive a written statement giving the reason for their dismissal. Where an employee is pregnant or absent from work on maternity leave, the right to a written statement of reasons for dismissal applies automatically without the employee having to make a request. Where such a request is made (whether verbally or in writing), the employer must comply with it within 14 days.

It is sound practice in any event to adopt a policy of providing all employees with a written statement outlining the reason for their dismissal, irrespective of length of service and whether or not a request has been made. The reason, or reasons, given should of course be true. If at a later date the employee presents a claim for unfair dismissal to an employment tribunal, the statement may be used in evidence. The reason(s) for dismissal quoted should tie in with one of the potentially fair reasons for dismissal (see above).

POTENTIAL REMEDIES FOR THE EMPLOYEE IF A CLAIM FOR UNFAIAR DISMISSAL SUCCEEDS

Where a claim for unfair dismissal succeeds, the tribunal may order one of the following remedies:

● Reinstatement;

● Re-engagement;

● Compensation.

In most successful cases of unfair dismissal the remedy is compensation.

Reinstatement and re-engagement

Reinstatement means re-employment in the same job from which the employee was dismissed, under the same contract of employment, and hence on the same terms and conditions that would have applied had the dismissal not taken effect.

Reinstatement will only be ordered where:

● The dismissed employee has requested it as a remedy; *and*

● The employment tribunal judges it appropriate to order reinstatement. This will depend, for example on whether it is practicable for the employer to take the employee back and whether the employee's conduct has rendered it inappropriate under the circumstances to make an order for reinstatement.

The tribunal will also award the employee a sum of money equivalent to net back pay plus the net value of any benefits to which the employee would have been entitled, but for the dismissal. This will be calculated so as to cover the period from the date of the dismissal up to the date of re-employment. The tribunal may also order certain deductions from the award of back pay if this is necessary in order to put the employee back in the position they would have been in but for the dismissal. There is no maximum on the amount payable under this heading.

170

Once reinstated, the employee's continuity of service is restored to what it would have been if the dismissal had not occurred, in other words the period during which the employee did not work for the employer is counted towards their continuous service with the employer.

Re-engagement means re-employment by the same employer on a new contract of employment. which may be on different terms from the old contract, but must not be substantially different or less favourable to the employee. Thus re-engagement is a more flexible remedy than reinstatement. A tribunal will normally only consider re-engagement where they decide that reinstatement is not suitable or possible. In other respects, the rules for ordering re-engagement are similar to those affecting reinstatement.

Compensation

Where neither reinstatement or re-engagement is sought or granted, the remedy will be compensation. This consists of two main elements, a basic award and a compensatory award.

The basic award

The basic award is calculated according to the same formula as statutory redundancy pay. The maximum payable at the time of writing is £9,900. This amount is reviewed annually in February each year. The formula is as follows:

Completed years of service	*Amount of payment for each year*
Years of service up to and including age 21	½ week's pay
Years of service between age 22 and 40 inclusive	1 week's pay
Years of service age 41 and over	1½ weeks' pay

A week's pay for the purposes of calculating the basic award has a ceiling of (currently) £330. Thus an employee who earned more than £330 per week would have their basic award calculated on the figure of £330 per week, whilst an employee whose earnings were below £330 per week would be granted a basic award calculated according to their actual weekly wages.

The basic award can be reduced (by a percentage or even to zero, where appropriate) in a range of circumstances, for example where the employee has already received a sum of money from the employer which is in excess of the total of the maximum basic and compensatory awards.

The compensatory award

The compensatory award does not depend on a fixed formula, but will be as much as the tribunal considers just and equitable in all the circumstances of the case, taking into account the financial loss suffered by the complainant. The current maximum is £63,000.

In calculating how much to award, the tribunal will take into account:

- Loss of wages and benefits from the date of the employee's dismissal up to the date of the tribunal hearing;

- Estimated future loss of earnings resulting directly from the dismissal if the employee has, by that time, still not found new employment at a comparable rate of pay;

- Expenses incurred in seeking new employment;

- Loss of statutory rights;

- Loss of pension rights.

There is no provision for the compensatory award to include an amount to cover injury to feelings or loss of job satisfaction, despite various vigorous attempts in recent years to argue this matter before the courts.

The tribunal may reduce the amount of the compensatory award in certain circumstances, including where the employee has earned money from a new job, to offset monies paid by the ex-employer, where the employee's actions caused or contributed to their dismissal, or where the employee has failed to mitigate their loss, i.e. refused, or failed to seek, new employment.

Refusal to Comply with a Reinstatement or Re-engagement Order

Although employment tribunals have the power to order reinstatement or re-engagement of an unfairly dismissed employee, they do not, paradoxically, have the power to enforce their own reinstatement or re-engagement orders. In effect, therefore, the employer is able to refuse to re-employ the individual despite an order for reinstatement or re-engagement issued by the tribunal.

The disadvantaged employee does, however, have an additional cause of action in these circumstances. Where the employer has failed or refused to comply with a reinstatement or re-engagement order within the time limit specified by the tribunal, the dismissed employee may return to the tribunal and claim an additional award of compensation. Such a claim will normally succeed unless the employer can satisfy the tribunal that it was not reasonably practicable for them to comply with the order. The additional award is a sum of money of between 26 – 52 weeks' pay, with a "week's pay" being capped at £330 (as is the case for the basic award). The current level of award is therefore a figure of between £8,580 and £17,160.

KEY POINTS

Managers should:

- Recognise that employees have the statutory right not to be dismissed unfairly.

- Refrain from pressurising an employee into resigning as this is usually construed as an express dismissal.

- Be prepared to cooperate with an ACAS conciliation officer to see whether there is a possibility of a settlement with an employee who is claiming unfair dismissal and, if appropriate, whether it might be feasible to reinstate or re-engage the dismissed employee.

- Consider whether it would be preferable to negotiate with an employee whom the manager wishes to dismiss in order to reach a compromise agreement, rather than risk facing a complaint of unfair dismissal at an employment tribunal.

- Note that any termination agreement reached privately between an employer and an employee that does not meet the stringent requirements of a compromise agreement will not be legally binding to prevent the employee taking a claim of unfair dismissal to tribunal.

- Recognise that, even if there is a solid reason to dismiss an employee that will not be sufficient on its own to ensure fairness in law, as the law also requires proper procedures to be followed.

- Take care not to let emotions such as anger and impatience get in the way of objective judgement when considering whether an employee's behaviour is sufficient to justify the penalty of dismissal.

- Make sure that the employer has in place a written disciplinary procedure and that the terms of the procedure are followed in all cases.

- Carry out a full and fair investigation into any alleged misconduct before considering dismissing the employee.

- Understand that an employer does not need to have proof beyond reasonable doubt of an employee's misconduct for a dismissal to be fair, as the three-part test used is that there must have been a genuine belief, based on reasonable grounds, after a thorough investigation that there was sufficient reason to dismiss the employee based on the facts known at the time.

- Before contemplating dismissal on the grounds of unsatisfactory performance, ensure that the employee has been given a full opportunity (and sufficient training and time) to improve to the required standard and fair warning that continuing unsatisfactory performance would lead to dismissal.

- Inform all employees in writing each time any change is made to the employer's disciplinary and/or grievance procedures.

- Recognise that dismissal for any one of a long list of reasons is prohibited and will be regarded in law as being automatically unfair.

- Make sure that any employee who is to be dismissed is given the correct amount of notice due to them under either statute or their contract of employment (whichever is the longer).

- Recognise that there is no right for the employer to withdraw notice to terminate a contract of employment once it has been given, nor any right to extend or shorten the notice period unless the employee agrees to the change or is paid for the outstanding portion of the notice period.

- Make sure that each employee's contract includes a clause giving the employer the authority to elect, at their discretion, to grant pay in lieu of notice rather than permitting the employee to work out their notice period.

- Consider whether to place an employee who is leaving the organisation on garden leave, which means paid leave of absence during which the employee, whilst not working, continues to be employed and thus remains bound by all the terms of their contract of employment.

- Make sure that whenever an employee is dismissed, their termination date is unequivocally stated in writing and the employee clearly informed that all obligations and entitlements under the contract will cease on that date.

- Adopt a policy of providing all employees with a written statement outlining the reason for their dismissal, irrespective of length of service and whether or not a request has been made for such a statement.

CHAPTER 9
MANAGING CHANGE

INTRODUCTION

There are many reasons why an employer may need or want to make changes to the way they run their businesses and/or to the terms and conditions on which their employees work. This chapter covers the processes that managers should engage in when change becomes necessary in order to avoid being in breach of employees' contracts. Dismissals other than for misconduct, unsatisfactory job performance and ill-health are also covered in this chapter, specifically the legality of dismissals for retirement, "legal restriction" and "some other substantial reason".

THE POTENTIAL DIFFICULTIES INVOLVED IN INSTITUTING CHANGE

It is a normal reaction for employees to fear change, or to be suspicious about management's plans to introduce change. The prospect of change brings uncertainty, and individuals often worry about how the change will affect them or whether they will cope adequately with a reorganisation of their department, new methods of working, different shift patterns, etc. Depending on whether or not there is a solid relationship of openness and trust between management and staff, the introduction of change may either be received in an atmosphere of cooperation or alternatively may be rigorously opposed all the way down the line.

The Legal Status of Employment Terms and Conditions

The first important point that managers should understand is that, once the terms of an employee's contract have been agreed, they cannot be unilaterally altered by the employer unless the employee's agreement to the particular change has first been obtained. This will be the case unless there is a pre-existing flexibility clause in the employee's contract allowing for defined changes.

For example a clause that states that the employer has the right to alter the employee's pattern of working hours. In the absence of such a flexibility clause, the manager, in this example, would have to obtain the employee's express agreement if they wished to implement a change to the employee's hours of work or shift pattern, otherwise the change would be in breach of contract.

Nevertheless, employers do, from time to time, have sound business reasons to restructure, reorganise or introduce changes to their methods of working, and these changes may in turn necessitate changes to the terms of employees' contracts. Courts and tribunals recognise that it is sometimes necessary for employers to change employment terms, depending on a range of circumstances that affect the business.

It is important, however, to proceed with any proposed changes in a reasonable and measured way, which in essence means embarking on a process of consultation with a view to seeking employees' agreement to the proposed changes.

HOW TO PROCEED WHEN THERE IS A NEED TO IMPLEMENT CHANGES TO EMPLOYEES' TERMS AND CONDITIONS

Where the manager wishes to alter one or more of the terms of employees' contracts, and where there is no authority contained within the contracts themselves for such a change, the manager will have to embark on a process of consultation aimed at securing the employees' agreement to the proposed change(s). This principle holds good whether the proposed changes affect one employee, a group of staff in a particular department or the whole workforce. Where a large number of employees will be affected by proposed changes, it is usual for the employer to consult with appointed representatives.

Implementing changes without consulting each affected employee and seeking their agreement is not an option, unless the manager wishes to give employees solid ammunition to take the employer to court. This is the case irrespective of the manager's views and opinions on the matter, and irrespective of how strongly or rightly the manager feels that contractual changes are necessary. A contract of employment is legally binding and it is not open to either party to change its terms without the agreement of the other.

The general principle inherent in change is that management should act reasonably towards employees. The key to success lies in open, meaningful, two-way consultation with a view to reaching agreement. Managers should therefore approach the issue in a rational, fair and patient manner and should never attempt to implement changes to contractual terms hastily.

Sound Business Reasons

The first principle in implementing change in employment terms is to examine the reasons behind the proposed changes, and analyse whether these reasons are genuinely related to the needs of the business. If the process of change is to succeed without the employer having to face legal claims from disgruntled employees, the changes must be shown to be linked to the achievement of a legitimate business aim. A change that is rooted in administrative convenience or personal preference is unlikely to amount to a sound business reason.

Consultation

The employer should embark upon a process of full consultation in relation to the proposed changes. Consultation may be with the representatives of a trade union (if one is recognised), an information and consultation committee or with individuals directly. Meetings should be held so that management can put forward their proposals, provide a full explanation for the reasons behind the proposals, answer any questions that employees may raise and give reassurances where appropriate. Often employees will cooperate with their employer provided they understand the reasons why changes are necessary, whereas keeping them in the dark is virtually guaranteed to create negative reactions and possibly even outright hostility.

Employees should be given the opportunity to put forward their views, suggestions and objections to the proposed changes. Management should consider these views, suggestions and objections, and subsequently be prepared to amend the proposals to accommodate them where it is practicable and reasonable to do so.

The proposed changes may also create problems for individual employees, for example an employee who has young children may be unable to vary their working hours so as to accommodate an earlier start time or a later finish time. Managers should be willing to meet individually with any employees who face particular problems and should take their circumstances into account. Furthermore, the manager should be open-minded and flexible enough to accommodate individuals' needs where it is possible to do so, for example by making an exception for the individual concerned.

Information and Consultation of Employees Regulations 2004

Since April 2005, employers with 150 or more employees are obliged (under the *Information and Consultation of Employees Regulations 2004*) to set up an information and consultation forum for employees upon request from at least 10 per cent of the workforce. The key purpose of the Regulations is so that employees may have the opportunity to be involved in any potential changes that affect their employment and influence management decisions.

The Regulations were extended to employers with 100 or more staff as from April 2007 and to those with 50 or more staff from April 2008.

Periods for consultation

An employer who embarks on a process of consultation with a view to instigating changes to employees' terms of employment should allow the same time periods for consultation as are applicable to collective redundancy consultation. This means:

● Beginning the consultation at least 30 days before any changes are finalised, when 20 or more employees at one establishment are likely to be affected by the changes;

● Beginning the consultation at least 90 days before any changes are finalised, where 100 or more employees at one establishment are likely to be affected.

The reason for this is to protect the employer in the event that employees have to be dismissed and re-employed in order to effect the desired changes (see below under "Termination of Existing Contracts and Offer to Re-employ"). Minimum periods of consultation are required in law as soon as an employer contemplates dismissing employees either by reason of redundancy or for any other reason not related to the individual.

Confirming the position in writing

Following consultations, the manager should send a letter to each employee, confirming the position and putting forward any revised proposals. The letters should ask employees to agree to the specific changes to the terms of their contracts of employment. If employees do agree to the changes at this stage, then the remaining steps detailed below under "Dealing with employees who refuse to agree" will not be required.

Keeping records

Full, written records should be kept of each part of the consultation process. Such records should document the proposals put forward, any suggestions or objections advanced by employees, any other options that have been explored and the reasons why other options have been rejected.

Where employees agree to the changes, the employer should write to each of them to confirm this fact (see "Confirming the Changes" below).

Dealing with Employees who Refuse to Agree to Changes

Even where an employer has followed through a full process of consultation with employees over proposed changes and has acted reasonably in doing so, this is of course no guarantee that employees will agree to the changes that the employer wants to implement.

Further individual consultation may be necessary with those employees who refuse or fail to agree to the changes put forward by management. Often the best way forward is for managers to meet with employees individually to talk openly about their reasons for not signing up to the proposed changes. In many cases the employee may simply need to have a particular point clarified, or may want further reassurance on a specific issue. Informal face-to-face meetings are often the best way to resolve such issues.

Warning of termination

If, despite management's best efforts, some employees still refuse to accept the proposed changes, the next step would be write to those employees to warn them that the consequence of their continuing refusal to agree to the changes will be termination of their existing contracts of employment (i.e. dismissal) and an offer of re-employment on revised terms. The manager should communicate this to each individual employee by letter, and, at the same time, offer one more opportunity for them to confirm their acceptance of the proposed changes by a date specified in the letter.

Termination of existing contracts and offer to re-employ

The final step, in the event that some employees continue to refuse to agree to the proposed changes, will be to proceed to introduce the changes by giving employees notice of termination of their current employment contracts (see chapter 8 for information on notice periods) and at the same time offering them re-employment on the new terms.

Employees should be informed clearly that if they accept the offer of re-employment, they will maintain their continuity of service. Indeed the letter offering re-employment should state that all the employee needs to do to accept the offer is to turn up for work on the next working day following the date of termination of their existing contract. This approach avoids the need for managers to insist on obtaining signatures from every employee to indicate agreement to the new terms. The fact that an employee has turned up for work and performed the contract under the new terms will be sufficient in law to indicate agreement.

Employees who decline to accept the new contract will, in effect, have been dismissed. This brings with it the risk of claims for unfair dismissal from those who have attained at least a year's service. If, however, the employer has followed the procedure outlined above, it is likely that any claims for unfair dismissal would not succeed, especially if the majority of employees have accepted the new terms. The reason for the dismissal would fall under the heading of "some other substantial reason" (see below).

This process is, of course, not risk-free, but it does avoid any risk of breach of contract claims, provided the notice given to terminate the employees' contracts complies with statutory and/or contractual notice entitlements (see chapter 8).

Introducing the changes without termination and re-employment

The alternative course of action is for the employer to follow through the process of consultation outlined above and then simply give employees notice that they intend to introduce the change(s) from a stated future date. This would technically allow employees who opposed the changes to regard the employer as being in breach of contract irrespective of the employer's efforts to act reasonably and engage in a consultation process. In order to avoid breach of contract claims therefore, the employer must either obtain employees' express agreement to the changes proposed, or else give notice to *terminate* the contract and not to *vary* its terms.

Introducing New Policies/Procedures

In instances where the proposed change involves the introduction of a new or revised policy or procedure, for example a computer use policy, termination of employees' contracts combined with an offer of re-engagement may or may not be necessary, depending on whether the policy forms (or is to form) part of employees' contracts with disciplinary sanctions being applied for non-compliance. Whether or not this is the case, there must be a sound business reason for the new policy, for example many employers would have introduced new or revised smoking policies following the legislation banning smoking at work implemented in England/Wales in July 2007 and in Scotland in March 2006.

If the new policy is to be regarded as a management guideline rather than a requirement of employees' contracts, the employer should:

- Communicate the detail of the proposed new policy/procedure to employees and fully explain the reasons why it is necessary from a business standpoint;

- Give employees a full opportunity to put forward their views, suggestions and objections to the new policy/procedure;

- Take those views into account before finalising the policy or procedure.

Once consultation has been carried out, the employer may notify employees of their intention to introduce the policy or procedure at a stated future date, giving reasonable notice (around three months as a minimum).

Further considerations would include the need to:

- Ensure the policy/procedure was clearly communicated in writing to all employees individually prior to its implementation.

- State clearly the consequences of any breaches of the new policy/procedure, i.e. whether a breach will constitute misconduct under the organisation's disciplinary procedure, and the likely penalties for such a breach. It is important that employees are fully informed of the likely penalties for refusing to comply with the new policy/procedure after its introduction, especially if they may be liable to be dismissed.

- Following introduction, ensure the policy or procedure is enforced fairly and consistently throughout the organisation.

Confirming the Changes

There is no requirement in law to re-issue a complete new contract of employment each time a change is made. Instead, once the change has been agreed, the employer is under a duty to notify the employee individually in writing of the contractual terms that have changed and the date from which the change is effective.

Such notification must be provided to each employee no later than four weeks after the date the change was implemented.

THE POSSIBLE ADVERSE CONSEQUENCES OF ACTION THAT AMOUNTS TO BREACH OF CONTRACT

Where the employer imposes a change to an employee's terms or conditions of employment without the employee's agreement, the employee may be able to take a number of courses of action against the employer. The employee may be entitled to:

- Refuse to work under the new terms;

- Resign and claim constructive dismissal;

- State they are continuing to work "under protest";

- Sue the employer for damages in an ordinary civil court;

- Where the change to employees' terms involves a pay cut, make a claim for unlawful deductions from wages.

Each of these is explored below.

A Refusal to Work under the New Terms

If new terms of employment introduced by management involve (for example) a change in hours or job duties, a refusal on the employee's part to work under the new terms would put management in the difficult position of having to start the process of consultation over again. If the employer was to dismiss an employee for refusing to work under new terms that had not been agreed, such a dismissal might possibly be judged fair (if the employer had fully followed the processes outlined above). It could also be unfair (if the employer had not done so, or if the employee had a justifiable reason for refusing to agree to the change). The outcome, of course, would depend on all the circumstances of the individual case and also on whether proper disciplinary procedures were followed in the run-up to the employee's dismissal.

Constructive Dismissal

Employees need a minimum of one year's continuous service to be eligible to claim constructive dismissal. Constructive dismissal claims are based on the assertion that the employer has breached one or more of the terms of the employee's contract and that the employee, as a result, feels that continued working for the employer is intolerable.

Other conditions for a claim for constructive dismissal to be valid are that:

- The breach of contract must be fundamental (i.e. not just be a minor or insubstantial change);

- The employee must be able to show that they resigned as a direct result of the breach of contract and not for some other reason; and

- The employee must have resigned promptly following the breach of contract, otherwise they will be deemed by implication to have agreed to the changes (see also below under "The Effect of the Employee Doing Nothing").

Continued Working under Protest

An employee faced with unwelcome changes to their contract may write to the employer making it clear that they have not agreed to the changes and that they are continuing to work "under protest". Any manager who receives such a letter from an employee should take the matter seriously and expect legal action to follow.

Suing the Employer for Damages

Where changes to an employee's contract involve a financial loss (for example a pay cut), the employee may elect to sue the employer in a civil court (not a tribunal) for breach of contract. No minimum period of service is required for this type of claim and the employee does not need to leave in order to proceed. There would, however, be no point from the employee's perspective in doing so unless the change had led to a significant financial loss.

A court in assessing a claim of this type will not be concerned with the reasonableness or otherwise of the employer's actions but will instead be interested in establishing the terms of the employee's contract, whether these had been altered without agreement and whether the employee had suffered any monetary loss as a result.

Unlawful Deductions from Wages

If the evidence is that the employer instituted a reduction to an employee's remuneration without the employee's advance written agreement, the employee will have a very good chance of succeeding in a claim for unlawful deductions from wages, simply by presenting their pay slips in evidence. No minimum period of service is required for a claim for unlawful deductions from wages, which is heard by an employment tribunal. Equally, the employee does not need to resign in order to bring this type of claim.

The Effect of an Employee Doing Nothing

If, following a change to the terms of the contract, the employee carries on working normally and takes no action to indicate any objection to the change, they will be taken to have accepted the new terms after a relatively short period of time.

There is, however, no defined time period after which an employee's acceptance of a change will be implied. Instead, what is relevant is whether it can be argued that the employee's actions are consistent with their having accepted the change. For example, if, following a cut to an employee's weekly rate of pay, the employee continued to work normally and at the end of the week accepted their weekly pay cheque, it could be argued that this behaviour constituted an acceptance of the pay cut after only a week (or two at the most).

This would be the case unless the employee had written to the employer indicating that they had not agreed to the pay cut and making it clear that they were continuing to work under protest.

Although it is obviously in the interests of every organisation to ensure that signed acceptance of any change is received from all employees who are affected, the absence of an employee's signature indicating acceptance will be inconsequential if the employee continues to work normally without expressing any formal objections.

This conduct, as stated above, will constitute an implied agreement to the change which, ultimately, has the same effect as a signed written agreement.

Other Possible Consequences of Imposing Unwelcome Changes

Even if there are no legal repercussions following management's introduction of change without employees agreement, managers may wish to consider the impact on morale and motivation inevitably created by unwelcome changes to working terms or conditions. The effects can be considerable, long-term and extremely damaging in respect of the organisation's productivity. Common effects include higher labour turnover, difficulties in recruitment, soaring rates of sickness absence, lower standards of performance, claims for workplace stress, etc.

Handling Employee Grievances

An employee who believes that their manager is attempting to introduce new and unwelcome terms of employment may choose to invoke the organisation's grievance procedure. The key purposes of any grievance procedure should be to allow employees to raise genuine workplace grievances openly and without fear of recrimination and to make genuine attempts to resolve those grievances in whatever way(s) are practicable and reasonable.

Grievances should always be dealt with promptly (not in haste, but rather within as short a timescale as is reasonably practicable) and wherever possible should be settled by the employee's immediate manager. The manager should set up a meeting with the employee to discuss the nature of the grievance and the reason(s) why the employee feels aggrieved. Following the meeting, it may be necessary to investigate the matter further in order to talk to colleagues, establish facts and review any relevant policies, rules or management guidelines. After deciding what (if any) action to take to deal with the employee's grievance, the manager should confirm this decision to the employee in writing. This should be done even if the decision is that the grievance has not been upheld, or if, despite being upheld, no action can realistically be taken. There should also be provision for a right of appeal to a more senior manager if the employee is dissatisfied with the manager's decision.

A further point to note is that employees have the statutory right, if they wish, to be accompanied at any formal grievance hearing by a fellow worker or trade union official of their choice (see also chapter 2, "The Right to be Accompanied at a Disciplinary Interview").

Many managers view the raising of grievances with trepidation, but in most cases there should be no cause for this. If an employee has a genuine grievance, it is clearly better for the manager to know about it so that steps can be taken to discuss the matter, understand the employee's point of view and if possible provide a remedy or even a compromise solution. A constructive approach therefore is to view the raising of grievances positively, as approaching a workplace problem with a positive attitude may enable it to be satisfactorily resolved. A negative attitude on the other hand is likely to alienate the employee and aggravate the situation. If the manager refuses to listen or take the employee's grievance seriously, or treats the employee as a trouble-maker, then the employee will now have two grievances – the original grievance which remains unresolved and the additional grievance about the manager's uncompromising and unhelpful attitude.

RETIREMENT AS A REASON FOR DISMISSAL

Since the implementation (in October 2006) of the *Employment Equality (Age) Regulations 2006*, age discrimination in employment has been prohibited and new retirement provisions have been in force for all employers. The regulations introduced provisions allowing employers to compel employee's aged 65 or over to retire and adding "retirement" to the list of potentially fair reasons for dismissal.

Age 65 is the standard, or default, retirement age. This does not mean, however, that an employer is required to retire employees at age 65, as there is no bar on the employment, or continued employment, of older people. The employer may therefore choose to do any of the following:

● Implement a policy of retiring all staff at age 65;

● Implement a policy of retiring staff at some higher age, for example age 70;

- Operate a flexible retirement policy, allowing staff to choose to retire between a stated lower and upper age limit;

- Operate without any retirement age and instead allow employees individually to decide when to stop working.

What the regulations do not permit, however, is compulsory retirement before age 65, unless a lower retirement age can be objectively justified in each individual case – which would almost certainly be extremely difficult, if not impossible, to achieve. An employer that wished to terminate an employee's employment before he or she reached the age of 65 would, realistically, have to have another potentially fair reason for dismissing the employee.

The retirement provisions introduced by the *Employment Equality (Age) Regulations* do not impact on voluntary retirement as no dismissal will have taken place in circumstances where an employee volunteers to retire.

Furthermore, the retirement provisions do not affect the age at which an employee may draw a state or occupational pension.

Mandatory Procedures for Retirement

As stated above, the retirement provisions in the *Employment Equality (Age) Regulations* made retirement a potentially fair reason for dismissal. As with all dismissals, however, the employer must follow certain procedures if the dismissal is to be fair. It is important to note that if the mandatory retirement procedures outlined below are not followed, the employee's dismissal by reason of retirement will be automatically unfair.

Notification

Special notification procedures apply to retirement dismissals. The employer must:

- Notify each employee whom they wish to retire in writing of their proposed retirement date at least six months (but not more than 12 months) in advance of that date. A retirement age contained in a policy, employee handbook or in the employee's contract will not suffice for this purpose.

- At the same time, notify the employee that they have the right, if they wish, to submit a written request to continue working beyond the retirement date notified by the employer.

- If the employee does submit a request to continue working, deal with the request in the manner described in the next sub-section.

Where an employer fails to inform an employee within the mandatory time-frame of their proposed retirement date and of their right to request to continue working beyond that date, the employee may bring a complaint to an employment tribunal. If the claim succeeds, the employee may be awarded up to eight weeks' pay as compensation.

The right to request to continue working

An employee who wishes to ask their employer to permit them to continue working beyond a retirement date notified to them must specify in writing exactly what they want, i.e. whether the request is to continue working indefinitely or for a defined limited period. The employee is under no obligation to provide any reason for the request.

Where an employee submits a request to continue working beyond their notified retirement date, the employer must follow a mandatory "duty to consider procedure". Under this procedure, the employer must:

- Set up a meeting with the employee within a reasonable period to discuss the request.

- Allow the employee, if they wish, to be accompanied at the meeting by a fellow worker of their choice.

- Be open-minded at the meeting and be prepared to discuss any viable options, for example the manager may propose alternatives to what the employee has requested such as a different (later) retirement date or a variation to the employee's working pattern or job duties if it is agreed that they should stay on.

- Provide a decision in writing as soon as possible after the meeting.

- If the request is granted, confirm what has been agreed in writing, including (if relevant) any later retirement date that has been agreed, for example if the employee wanted to work on only for a limited period.

- If the request is subsequently refused, grant a right of appeal and, if the employee does appeal, ensure the appeal is heard by a different (and preferably more senior) manager from the one who took the decision to refuse the employee's request.

If the employer is prepared to agree immediately to the employee's request, then there is no need to hold a formal meeting. In this case, confirmation of the agreement should nevertheless be put in writing and a copy given to the employee.

The employer is not obliged to justify a refusal to agree to an employee's request to continue working beyond retirement age. Strangely, there is not even any legal duty on the employer to tell the employee the reason for the refusal, although it would represent good practice to do so.

Where the employer agrees to an employee's request to continue working that does not prevent the employer from retiring the employee at some future date. The retirement procedures can be invoked again at any time.

Where an employee works on beyond age 65, they continue to be protected by employment legislation in the normal way, including the continuation of the right not to be subjected to age discrimination. In other words, an employee who works on beyond age 65 must not be treated any differently from younger staff on any grounds related to age, unless the employer can objectively justify the different treatment.

The case of *Martin v SS Photay and Associates [2007] ET 1100242/07* demonstrates the dangers of assuming that an employee past retirement age can be dismissed arbitrarily or treated differently on grounds of age. Soon after Ms Martin, who worked as a cleaner in a dental surgery, had reached her 70th birthday, she received a letter from her employer saying "... due to your age and health problems, you have fallen into the high risk category for health and safety. We cannot allow you to continue cleaning at the practice because of you being high risk". Ms Martin, having in effect been dismissed, consequently brought a claim to tribunal for age discrimination.

The employment tribunal upheld her claim – it was somewhat obvious that age was one of the prime reasons for her dismissal since the letter had specifically mentioned her age. The tribunal also considered it relevant that the employer had not obtained any medical evidence about Ms Martin's health to support its assertion that she fell into a high-risk category. Instead, they had just made an assumption about it.

Interestingly, the employer in this case could have fairly and lawfully terminated Ms Martin's employment by reason of retirement, if they had followed the mandatory pre-retirement procedures.

"LEGAL RESTRICTION" AS A REASON FOR DISMISSAL

"Legal restriction" (sometimes referred to as "statutory bar") occurs where the continued employment of a particular employee in the job they are employed to do would contravene the law. Examples include situations in which:

- An employee engaged as a driver, or one whose job necessitates driving, loses their driving licence (see below);

- It is discovered that an employee of foreign nationality is working illegally;

- A foreign employee's right to remain in the UK runs out and cannot be extended or renewed;

- An employee who needs to hold a particular qualification in order to be able to practise their job or profession fails to gain the qualification, or loses it through disbarment;

- The employment of a young person contravenes statutory provisions, for example if it is discovered that someone working in licensed premises is under the age of 18;

- The continuation of a particular person's employment would contravene health and safety regulations.

As with all dismissals, fairness will depend on whether the employer has acted reasonably in dismissing the employee for the reason given. This will depend on whether fair and reasonable procedures have been followed. Reasonableness in dismissing an employee on the grounds of legal restriction will depend on a number of factors:

- Whether the ban affects the whole of the employee's job, or just part of it;

- The likely duration of the statutory ban if it is temporary;

- Whether the employee has been dishonest, for example by failing to disclose material facts.

The key factor determining fairness will be whether dismissal was the only reasonable option open to the employer in all the circumstances, i.e. dismissal should only be a last resort once other options have been explored such as:

- Whether the employee could be transferred to another job (whether temporarily or permanently);

- Whether the employee's job duties could be altered;

- Whether any other arrangements are feasible.

Managers should also make sure they adopt an open-minded attitude and fully consult an employee about all possible courses of action, rather than taking a unilateral decision as to what action to take.

Where a Driver Loses their Driving Licence

The most common type of dismissal on the grounds of legal restriction is one in which an employee whose job by necessity involves driving loses their driving licence. When this occurs, the manager should give the employee an opportunity to express their views about how to resolve the situation and consider the following matters to establish what reasonable courses of action might be possible:

- The duration of the driving ban, for example if it is quite short it may be possible to transfer the employee temporarily into another job;

- The reason for the ban, for example whether it was as a result of a drink-driving offence, or some factor outside the employee's control (for example diagnosis of a medical condition that means that the employee is not allowed to drive);

- To what extent driving is an essential part of the employee's job;

- Whether the employee's contract includes a provision that the employee must be able to drive.

The employer should be willing to consider any reasonable suggestions put forward by the employee as to how the situation might be resolved without the need for the employee to be dismissed.

Even if there is a clause in the employee's contract or in the organisation's disciplinary rules that an employee engaged as a driver will automatically be dismissed if they lose their driving licence, this will not necessarily be sufficient to make a dismissal on these grounds fair. Fairness will always require a consideration of whether other courses of action are feasible in the circumstances, with dismissal being viewed as a last resort. There may be a number of possible ways of retaining the employee despite the loss of their licence:

- The employee providing (at their own cost) a "chauffeur" for the duration of the ban;

- The employee using public transport or taxis to travel on company business;

- Another employee being asked to drive the employee to and from business appointments;

- Transferring the person's driving duties to another employee on a temporary basis.

"SOME OTHER SUBSTANTIAL REASON" AS A REASON FOR DISMISSAL

"Some other substantial reason" (SOSR) is one of the potentially fair reasons for dismissal listed in the *Employment Rights Act 1996*. SOSR is defined as "a reason of a kind such as to justify the dismissal of an employee holding the position which the employee held". This in effect allows employers to seek to justify dismissing an employee for a reason that does not fall within any of the other potentially fair categories, provided only that the reason is "substantial" and not trivial. SOSR is thus effectively a "catch-all" category allowing employers to justify a dismissal that has taken place for a substantial reason.

There is no list of reasons defined in statute that may fall under the category of SOSR, but over the course of many years employment tribunals have developed precedents as to what reasons might be regarded as "substantial" and reasonable under this heading. Technically any reason may be put forward, so long as it is sufficient (when viewed objectively) to justify dismissal. Claims of unfair dismissal under the heading of SOSR require the employer to show that they followed proper procedures and acted reasonably, as is the case for all dismissals.

Some of the substantial reasons which have been accepted by tribunals as potentially fair under SOSR include:

- An employee's refusal to agree to new terms and conditions of employment that are necessary in light of a business reorganisation (see above under "Dealing with Employees who Refuse to Agree to Changes");

- A potential breach of trust or confidentiality which may arise in a range of circumstances, including where an employee is in a close personal relationship with someone employed by a competitor company;

- A severe personality clash between two employees which is having a serious effect on the work and which cannot be resolved in any other way;

- Pressure from a client or customer (see below);

- The return to work of an employee following an absence (for example maternity leave) resulting in the dismissal of a temporary employee who was engaged to cover their absence (provided the temporary employee had been informed in writing in advance that their employment would terminate in these circumstances);

- Inappropriate conduct outside of work which impacts in some way on the employee's employment;

- Imprisonment of the employee;

- An employee's failure to disclose relevant information in an application for employment, transfer or promotion, e.g. relevant medical history or lack of qualifications.

Pressure from a Customer or Client to Dismiss an Employee

If a customer or client exerts pressure on a manager to remove a particular employee from a project, contract or particular job, then the dismissal of the employee in question may be fair under the heading of SOSR. Fairness will, however, depend on a range of circumstances. A manager facing this type of situation should do the following:

- Review whether there is any contractual right for the customer to approve or disapprove the recruitment or continued employment of staff;

- Consider whether compliance with the customer's wishes is important to the business, i.e. whether there would be any serious negative consequences as a result of non-compliance;

- Take all reasonable steps to discuss the matter with the customer to establish the reason for their dissatisfaction with the particular employee and whether the matter can be resolved in any other way;

- Make reasonable attempts to find alternative work for the employee elsewhere within the organisation rather than dismiss them;

- Check whether the employee's contract contains a statement informing them that they may dismissed at the request of a customer (without such a clause, dismissal for this reason is likely to be unfair);

- Discuss the matter with the employee with a view to finding a solution other than dismissal;

- Take into account any injustice that may be caused to the employee if they are dismissed;

- Act reasonably towards the employee, and follow proper procedures if dismissal is to be implemented.

In order for this type of dismissal to be fair, the pressure on the manager need not amount to an outright demand to dismiss the employee or be as strong as a threat to withdraw business if the person is not dismissed. It may be sufficient to have received a complaint from a customer that the standard of work or conduct of a particular employee is unsatisfactory. It will, of course, be important in such circumstances to give the employee a full opportunity to respond to any complaints that have been made against them prior to deciding on what action to take (see chapter 4, "Dealing with Complaints from Customers about an Employee").

KEY POINTS

Managers should:

- Recognise that, once the terms of an employee's contract have been agreed, managers cannot unilaterally alter those terms unless the employee's consent to any proposed change is obtained.

- Proceed with any proposed changes to employees' terms and conditions in a reasonable and measured way by embarking on a process of consultation with a view to seeking employees' agreement to the changes.

- Make sure that there is a sound business reason behind any proposal to alter employees' terms and conditions of employment.

- Take into account the circumstances of any individual who is unable to comply with proposed changes to the terms of their employment and be flexible enough to accommodate their needs where it is possible to do so.

- Keep full, written records of the consultation process.

- Meet individually with any employees who decline to agree to the changes put forward by management in order to establish the individual's reason for not signing up to the proposed changes and clarify any particular issues that are of concern to the employee.

- Where employees continue to refuse to agree to new terms that are necessary for the business, proceed to introduce the changes by giving employees notice of termination of their current employment contracts and at the same time offering them re-employment on the new terms.

- Ensure any new policy is clearly communicated in writing to all employees individually, that the consequences of any breaches of the new policy are clearly stated and that adequate notice is given of the policy's introduction.

- Once a change to an employee's contract has been agreed, notify the employee in writing within four weeks of the terms that have changed and the date from which the changes are effective.

- Recognise the potential adverse legal and practical consequences of imposing contractual changes on an employee without the employee's prior agreement.

- Deal with any grievances raised by employees by discussing the matter with the employee at a meeting, investigating the matter further if necessary, giving fair consideration to ways in which the situation might be resolved and allowing a right of appeal.

- View the raising of grievances positively, as approaching a workplace problem with a positive attitude may enable it to be satisfactorily resolved.

- Understand that it is not permitted in law, unless there are exceptional circumstances, to compel an employee to retire before they have reached age 65.

- When seeking to retire an employee, ensure the mandatory notification and "duty to consider" procedures are fully applied.

- If information comes to light to suggest that it would be illegal to continue to employ a particular individual, ensure the individual is treated fairly and reasonably prior to dismissal.

- Only dismiss an employee on the grounds of legal restriction if dismissal is the only reasonable option in all the circumstances.

- In the event that an individual employed in a driving job loses their driving licence, give the person an opportunity to express their views about how to address the situation and consider all possible options other than dismissal.

- If dismissal is being considered for an SOSR dismissal ("some other substantial reason"), make sure that the reason in question is sufficient, when viewed objectively, to justify dismissal.

- If a customer exerts pressure on a manager to remove a particular employee from a project, contract or particular job, take all reasonable steps to discuss the matter with the customer, and with the employee, to establish whether any course of action other than dismissal is possible.

Author Profile

Lynda Macdonald has worked for over 15 years as a freelance trainer, advisor and writer specialising in employment law, and she regularly designs and conducts training courses on all aspects of employment law. She also sits as a panel member for the Employment Tribunals service. Previously, Lynda worked as an HR Manager in the oil industry for over ten years. She is a university graduate in language, a Chartered Fellow of the Chartered Institute of Personnel and Development and has a master's degree in employment law and practice. Lynda has written twelve previous books on various aspects of employment law, and co-authored several others, and she currently contributes extensively to various HR and employment law hardcopy and on-line products.

Lynda's personal interests include travel to remote and unusual places, digital photography, genealogy, gardening, and two small dogs.

Contact Lynda at: lyndamacdonald@clara.co.uk
or visit her website at: www.lyndamacdonald.co.uk